CONFESSIONS
of a
CAMO QUEEN

KRISTEN BERUBE

D1469090

FARCOUNTRY
PRESS

To my ever-encouraging, camo-clad,
nature-crazy husband, and best friend, Remi.
Thank you for a life full of laughter.

ISBN: 978-1-56037-628-6

© 2015 by Farcountry Press
Text © 2015 by Kristen Berube

Camo pattern design used on the front cover and throughout the book by Robert Rath.
Camo pattern design used on the inside front and inside back covers by Mark Lewis.

For more information about our books, write Farcountry Press, P.O. Box 5630,
Helena, MT 59604; call (800) 821-3874; or visit www.farcountrypress.com.

Library of Congress Cataloging-in-Publication Data

Berube, Kristen, 1982-
  Confessions of a camo queen / Kristen Berube.
     pages cm
  Summary: "Humorous stories from the perspective of an outdoorsman's
partner"-- Provided by publisher.
  ISBN 978-1-56037-628-6 (pbk.)
1. Outdoorsmen--Humor. 2. Masculinity--Humor. 3. Man-woman
relationships--Humor. 4. Berube, Kristen, 1982- I. Title.
  PN6231.O965B47 2015
  818'.602--dc23

                    2015015148

 Produced and printed in the United States of America.

19 18 17 16 15   1 2 3 4 5

CONTENTS

LIFE WITH A CAMO GUY

Hunting? Fishing? Hiking? Camping? Talking about hunting. Talking about fishing. Talking about camouflage. Talking about trucks. Talking about big bucks and big bulls....Does this sound like your life? Mine too. I am married to an outdoorsman.

My outdoorsman is into just about every sort of hunting or fishing that there is. To say the least, I hear about it a lot. I laugh at him daily.

Truth be told, I think that hunting and fishing are wonderful activities that keep people active, healthy, and out of low-life bars. I'd prefer that my outdoorsman hunt and fish rather than sit on the couch and drink a six-pack every night or go get hammered at the bar with his buddies. Granted, there are definitely those beer slammin' times too, but they generally involve campfires or football. I am grateful for hunting and fishing because not only do they get the guy out of my hair so I can go shopping without him nagging at me, "Are we done yet?" but I also appreciate all of the hormone-free, natural food we gain from his expeditions. Also because all that hiking keeps my man's booty firm! Rarrrr!

I gotta tell you though, being married to an outdoorsman is not without its trials and tribulations. Mostly, I just have to laugh at the crazy guy. I once was told, if you cannot laugh at all your significant other's quirks they will just drive you crazy. So since I don't want to end up in a straightjacket drooling, I embrace the wacko. Yes, he is an outdoors wacko.

From the incessant bugling practice, to the forgotten dead fish in the cooler in August, to the special hunting-scented laundry soaps and his habit of reading hunting magazines while perched on the throne for an hour at minimum, I just have to laugh. And keep laughing when I really just want to strangle the camouflage-clad man.

I wish there were something that made me as giddy as a school girl on a daily basis as hunting and fishing does for him. Yes, I have hobbies I love. I even enjoy going fishing and camping. I have to admit though, there's nothing I would repeatedly get up for every weekend at 4 a.m., freeze to death, rub my body down in estrus stink, snort and snuffle like a wild animal in public, spend every spare cent I have on a new camouflage pattern, or be willing to eat gas station corn dogs day in, day out. Hunting and fishing are his passion and I am grateful for them, but I just gotta share the crazy little nuances that make up an outdoorsman.

If you have an outdoorsman in your life, you'll likely appreciate knowing that you are not alone! There is a special club that all of us belong to. This elite, women-only club is called the Camo Queens. This year-round club becomes extremely active as soon as the calendar rolls around to September and the outdoorsmen turn their attention to bows and arrows. Our credit cards have been impatiently waiting for a workout while the outdoorsmen froth at the mouth, lusting for hunting season to begin once again. Yes, throughout the summer they go fishing and hiking, but nothing compares to the hell-bent fury that overwhelms outdoorsmen when they know that it is now big-game season. God help us all.

I am grateful for the encouragement and giggling my outdoorsman has given me while writing this book. When I read him a new chapter, he laughs and hides his face in his hands. He loves to hear how I see the crazy antics that he considers just plain normal. Wait, what part of rubbing elk estrus all over you is normal? As I was writing this book, he read along, remarking on his favorite sections. He even pretended to act embarrassed about some of it. Of course, he loves the camouflage lingerie chapter the best because it gets him thinking about women and underwear. Men!

Welcome to the world of the Camo Queen.

A CAMO QUEEN GLOSSARY

When I first fell for my ruggedly handsome outdoorsman, I had no idea that he spoke a foreign language. No, not a language of romance like Italian or French, and nothing as exotic as Balinese or Icelandic. Alas, his patois is more of a mashup of grunts, animal mating calls, pantomimes, and words shortened beyond recognition, except to dogs. The following glossary explains these sounds, and also the terms of endearment familiar only to Camo Queens.

Binos: a visual aid used to determine the species of ear mite infesting the hunter's prey across the valley and two ridges away. (See also Glassin'.)

Bite: when a sad little fish sacrifices itself to boost the outdoorsman's self-esteem; the slightest nibble causes symptoms of screaming, hooting, jumping up and down, and swearing. Side effects include swooning, sudden clumsiness, and tunnel vision. The ability to discern size becomes severely impaired, especially if the fish gets away.

Blind: a damp, icy tomb disguised as a cozy nest that you sit or lay in—dead still—waiting to convert innocent waterfowl into pillow filling.

Bugle: frickin' annoying $40 piece of plastic vacuum permanently affixed to the outdoorsman 365 days a year. He blows into the mouthpiece to make ear-shattering, never-ending screeches, alleged to imitate the mating calls of elk or a lonely, sex-starved Sasquatch. Occasionally used outdoors.

Call: A truly remarkable array of grunts, snorts, whistles, whinnies, howls, squawks, and squeals produced by the same outdoorsman whose conversational vocabulary is limited to "Beer," and "Uh-huh." Indistinguishable from normal male vocalizations made in the bathroom or bedroom. Upon hearing such calls, wild animals die laughing.

Camo: any article of clothing covered in a pattern designed to blend in seamlessly with grass, bushes, trees, wood, dirt, snow, or water, rendering the wearer magically invisible only to other outdoorsmen. Also worn as a badge of honor at the mall, four-star restaurants, and church.

Doggin': an expression of readiness to hunt—rapid pelvic thrusts made by the outdoorsman at inanimate objects, such as his 4-wheeler, much like a dog dry humping a pile of dirty laundry. Do NOT ask your outdoorsman for further explanation—it would be even more disturbing than the doggin' itself.

European Mount: outdoorsman art—a bleached skull of a wild animal, usually with horns attached. Despite 10,000 years of civilization, the outdoorsman will attempt to display such mounts as home décor in the dining room and over the master bed. Not to be mistaken for a position from the French Kama Sutra.

Glassin': using binos or a scope to scan every blade of grass on every distant slope, hoping to spot the massive buck that simply has to be there. Glassin' is a year-round form of Obsessive-Compulsive Disorder, not confined to hunting season. The older and dirtier the glass, the better the chance of spotting bears, coyotes, and trophy deer that to the untrained eye appear to be boulders, tree stumps, and shrubbery, respectively.

Hawg: any large, trophy-size animal, including hunting partners and girlfriends.

Honey Hole: a special, secret hunting spot rumored to hold monster bucks. Often indistinguishable from the surrounding landscape, which leads many hunters to wander aimlessly for days seeking the honey hole. (See also Lost.)

Hunting Widows Club: a sorority for all of us sisters who are seasonally abandoned by our paleo-camo guys while they romance furry critters and bed down with ticks, leeches, and intestinal parasites.

Lost: an unattainable state—no true-blooded outdoorsman has ever been lost. As Daniel Boone himself once said, "I have never been lost, but I will admit to being confused for several weeks."

Outdoorsman: a man obsessed with fishing, hunting, hiking, and otherwise wallowing in raw nature; a Neanderthal in $700 worth of designer camouflage.

Rack: the object an outdoorsman can't wait to get his hands on; the shapely, ample, uplifted, unrestrained, post-pubescent growth prominently displayed by male deer, elk, and moose—and female humans.

Rut: the time of year when deer, elk, and other critters produce excess hormones in preparation for procreation. The hormones stimulate outdoorsmen to act all horny and brainless around guns and 4-wheelers. (See also Doggin'.)

Sneak Attack: the act of the outdoorsman dressing up in the appropriate landscape camouflage and tiptoeing, bellycrawling, or teleporting close enough to the poor little bastard animal that he has locked his glazed-over eyes on, just before breaking wind and scaring the target into the next county.

Spot: Any highly secret location where the outdoorsman hunts, fishes, stalks, or otherwise harasses wildlife. Only the outdoorsman knows where these spots are, and he's gone to great pains to hide them from his buddies, Google Maps, the National Security Agency, Navy Seals Team Six, and you. Even his dog is blindfolded before driving to a spot.

Stink Wagon: the outdoorsman's vehicle, most likely a truck, with dog-hair seat covers and stale fart air fresheners. The wagon is a mobile Superfund site, full of rotten fossilized corn dogs, bloody feathers, random ungulate body parts, and more weapons than the National Guard. Do not enter without full hazmat protection.

White-knuckling: an instinctive, prehensile, female reflex triggered by engine revving, sudden braking, and violent swerving, common while the driver is hunting or glassin' from a vehicle.

PUPPY LOVE

Have you ever noticed that an outdoorsman in a truck always has a dog perched in the front seat? I seriously did not know that you could buy a pickup truck accessorized with a dog! Of course, the dog gets to ride shotgun, while the woman sulks in the backseat stuffed between the decoys and guns.

The bond between an outdoorsman and his dog is one that cannot be broken. Their love survives through thick and thin, through rain, snowstorms, crotch-deep mud, skunks, and porcupines. They are not merely a man and a dog; they are partners, brothers, each ready to risk everything for the other. If a wild bear attacks the man, the dog will dive right in, fangs bared. If the entire batch of fresh croissants disappears from the kitchen counter, including the foil, the man will take the fall for his brother. It's their code. These two will have each other's back no matter what.

You can see demonstrations of their love from the inch-thick layer of fur on the front seat of the truck to the unwavering love and attention in the dog's eyes as he looks at his outdoorsman. There is not a truck ride, a mountain climb, or even a night's sleep these two will spend apart. They speak the same language and share the same customs, from marking their territory to licking each other's faces. I tell you, if it weren't for dinner and a movie once in a blue moon, a woman could get jealous.

INSIDE THE CAMO GUY'S TRUCK

D o you know what stink is? I'm not sure you do, unless you have a camo guy in your life. There are so many stinky things involved with outdoorsmen that these guys should just come equipped with nose plugs for their poor, suffering women! The scary part is that the guys do not smell anything wrong. How is that even possible?

Mind you, we're not talking the mild, almost endearing aromas of sweaty gym clothes or nacho-cheese-and-beer burps. No, this is a full-on dumpster diving stench that makes flies swoon and turkey vultures circle overhead.

One of the stinkier areas of an outdoorsman is his truck. Oooooooweeeeeeeee, these things are ripe! The stank is so freaking rotten and overpowering that even a maggot would gag before the camo guy registers that his stink wagon might need to be cleaned.

The stink wagon is where it all happens, I am told— an outdoorsman's command central. Which means that the cab reeks from years of spilled coffee, stale donuts, petrified gas station burritos, and half-eaten corn dogs. But those trifles don't begin to explain where-oh-where that steaming stink comes from. If you could bottle that smell, I swear you'd have the ultimate weapon for chemical warfare. When you open the stink wagon's doors on a sweltering summer day, the odor hits like a bomb that will blow you back ten feet onto your keister. Or you just might asphyxiate right there in the open door. Death by stink—lucky me.

I'm telling you, I have cleaned out my camo guy's rig with a fine-toothed comb, I've had it professionally detailed, and I should own stock in vehicle air fresheners with how many I've hung on the rear-view mirror, but nothing works. You might as well dab deodorant on a pig—you can't mask that stink. Nasty, nasty, nasty.

On the occasions that I am forced to ride in the stink wagon, I crank the window down all the way and hang my head out like a stink-crazed hound dog. If you don't have the window down, you will go crazy trying to escape the stink. You can actually feel your sinuses pucker.

What could this stink be? Swamp muck? Wet dog? Rotten food? I have found some very interesting "food" crammed under the seats in Ziploc bags. At least I assume it used to be food. After months in the hot truck, it's just bags of slimy green and blue compost. Do NOT make the mistake of opening one of these bags! They don't make an antibiotic strong enough to cure you.

My camo guy's truck holds the recipe for stink soup: one part "scents" made from elk and deer pee, two parts floor mats soaked in last year's beer, and a dash of whatever dead animal the dog rolled in on the last trip. Stir in hot farts lingering in the upholstery and blend. Gross! I probably don't want to know the truth behind all those smells.

What I do know is that if I don't want to pass out from the fumes, wallow in dog fur, and smell like roadkill myself, I have to ride with my head out the window, wearing a poor-woman's hazmat suit made from a rain slicker and duct tape! The stench in that truck was so bad last summer—the sun beating down on the old rig, cooking up such a rancid funk—I started shopping for full-face respirators. Damn, those things are expensive! So instead, I found an old pair of earplugs, you know, those bright orange squishy foam ones that you roll up and insert? Turns out they fit in your nostrils just fine. I'll warn you though—you want to leave a little foam sticking out so you can remove them without too much fuss. And I guess it looks kind of odd. I forgot I had the plugs in my nose one day when we stopped at a Starbucks, and it's amazing how rude people can be, staring and pointing. You'd think it was the first time they'd ever seen a Camo Queen.

AN ELKAHOLIC BEHIND THE WHEEL

If extreme roller coasters make you queasy, be warned: never get in the camo guy's truck. Especially if he's in the mood to look for wild critters. A camo guy behind the wheel with deer or elk on his mind makes for a butt-puckering ride. And who are we kidding? A camo guy is always looking for elk, deer, shed horns, big furry critters, little furry critters, and anything with an open season on it. Like an astronaut on the launch pad, you have to have the right stuff to face a ride with the camo guy driving.

Your face will freeze in a silent, open-mouthed scream, your fingernails will dent four inches deep into the dashboard, and the ratcheting seatbelt will dislocate your pelvis. It's the wildest ride at the amusement park, but the risks are real. Newspaper stories about car wrecks always say, "Investigators have not yet determined whether alcohol and speed were factors," but they never print the truth: Billy Bob rolled the truck three times because he was scoping a big buck on that hillside two miles away while doing sixty across the washboards and trying not to spill his coffee.

It doesn't matter if there's no wild game within 150 miles. And it doesn't have to be hunting season. When a camo guy wants to go spotting, nothing will stop him. Of course, he'll spot the trophy rack or the huge bear even if no one else sees it. And for him, that makes all the chaos—

dodging trees and oncoming traffic, careening into the ditch, and overcorrecting—worthwhile.

Best of all is when he sees ducks or geese. Then out come the calls—small wooden mouthpieces designed to torture unsuspecting passengers in his vehicle. At the sight of a single duck, the camo guy jams a call into his mouth and starts trumpeting through it like Kenny G on methamphetamines. You've never heard such a ruckus! Quacks and squawks and squeals, all at ear-shattering volume. Seriously, those aren't rock chips in the windshield—it's cracked from the duck call shockwave! I don't know how one man can generate so many quacks all at once like that. The sheer volume of noise liquefies my brain and gives me nosebleeds. The camo guy is immune to the cacophony, of course, as are the ducks and geese. They pay no attention at all to the speeding Dodge pickup careening their way, honking louder than a whole flock of mallards. Which makes the camo guy squawk even louder into the call until I'm cross-eyed. Maybe he thinks he can stun the ducks if he just blows loud enough. Like the duck call is a sonic weapon. Lord knows it's given me a whole new sense of what it means to be within "earshot."

Despite all this, I frequently place my fate in the hands of my camo guy to go on a hair-raising, gut-sucking, wild ride in the stink wagon. I calmly buckle up, brace my legs in a wide vee, fiercely grab the "oh shit" handle, and I am ready to go. Once the outdoorsman buckles up, we're off. He punches the gas, he slams the brakes, we swerve, we screech to stops, we veer right, we veer left. The blast of wind from the open windows helps keep me conscious. Of course the windows are down the entire time because that see-through stuff—you know, the glass—well, it gets in the way, blocking our view. Really? Yep. It doesn't matter if it's 101 degrees out or below zero in a blizzard, those dang see-through windows must be down!

Whenever we go driving, we must have some sort of spotting mechanism with us, in every vehicle, at all times. There are mini binoculars shoved in the seat cushions, a rangefinder in the glove box, binos as big as bull testicles on the dash, and an ultra-spendy zoom spotting scope on a clamp that mounts to the driver's window. It's impossible to go three blocks to the store for milk without some sort of device to help him see up the backside of the local critters.

God forbid there's a deer a half mile away that we can't reach out and touch with our eyeballs. My question is, what is the outdoorsman looking for? Does he really need to count the fleas on every damn deer's ass? Does he need to look into the deer's eyes to know this is "the one" he'll stalk in three months? All while driving thirty miles an hour over the speed limit, running stop signs, and using the sidewalk as a passing lane?

Oh, it can't be that bad, you say? Just wait. Just wait till the nice neighbor lady knocks on your door Sunday morning to complain about the tire tracks in her flowerbed. Just wait till you have to untangle someone else's clothesline from the truck's antenna. Just wait till the day you start keeping Pepto-Bismol in the glove box. Just wait till you start swilling the Pepto like Jack Daniels to ease the butterflies in your stomach. Just wait till you need a prescription laxative to unclench the butt pucker six hours after surviving yet another Sunday drive. I swear, Disneyland should have a ride this wild.

Let's go for a spin, shall we? First, ease yourself into the stink wagon. I know, the thought of entering that reeking vehicle of filth triggers your fight-or-flight reflex, but you can do this. That burning in the back of your throat? Oh never no mind, that's normal. It's because you just threw up a little thanks to the rank aroma swirling throughout the truck. Have a seat. Don't bother trying to brush away the matted dog hair—think of it as extra padding for the beating you're about to take. Now buckle up—sorry, it's just the standard lap and shoulder belt. I know, it really should be the full-body harness like NASCAR drivers wear, but hey, what do you expect in a fifteen-year-old rusted-out Dodge? Sorry, there's no helmet, and we're not sure the passenger air bag works after being deployed so many times.

Whoa Nelly! Hang on! This is where your previous experience riding the mechanical bull down at the Busted Bronc Bar comes in handy. Yep, while you were relaxing into your seat, the outdoorsman hopped in, started her up, and popped the clutch. The G-forces are harsh, eh? Think of it as training for a NASA rocket launch. And don't worry about those footprints you're leaving on the dashboard—I brace my legs that way, too, in a futile attempt at keeping my butt in the seat. Now just relax, like you're at the gynecologist.

Ha! Oh, ouch! I should've warned you about those sudden sideways jerks. It's no fun when your head bounces off the doorframe like that. But hang in there, we're almost out of the driveway.

Which is about when he says, "Time to blow the carbon off the ol' valves," and he stomps the gas pedal, the tires scream, blue smoke fills the cab, and some guy on the radio is singing about his favorite fishing hole with the volume at ten.

Honest, the outdoorsman isn't trying to kill you, these are just his normal driving skills. Pay no mind to the windows rolling down— he's just making sure you don't miss any wildlife out there. I know, I know, it's hard to spot a deer while your head's ricocheting around the cab like a hockey puck, but that's the whole reason you were invited on this ride. Your job is to spot critters and call them out to the driver so he can glass them to decide which ones he wants to shoot in three months. Now pay attention, because you must do this in the right sequence—correctly identify the species, then which side of the road the critter is on, then distance. It should sound like this: "DEER! Right! 100 yards! ELK! Left! 50 yards!" In reality, I don't know how the outdoorsman sifts this information out of the random terrified screaming coming from the passenger seat, but somehow he manages. Also, for reasons unknown to womankind, despite asking us to spot animals for them, our camo guys don't find it helpful when you shout out other sightings, such as "SCHOOL BUS! Left! Way too close!" or "BRIDGE ABUTMENT! Straight ahead! Twenty feet and closing!"

The weird thing is, the camo guy doesn't bat an eye while I'm screaming bloody murder because I'm scared out of my freaking mind. That's normal driving mode for him. But the split second I shout "Deer!" his head whips around, the binos come flying out, and he's on the poor critter faster than a rat on a stray Cheeto.

If you think the ride's been rough so far, now's a good time to start praying. I hope you've also been doing lots of core muscle exercises—your abs and obliques are about to get a killer workout. The moment you've called his attention to a critter, the outdoorsman goes into hyperdrive. With his right hand he downshifts, usually skipping at least two gears. Meanwhile, his left hand rummages through the debris, desperately hunting for the binos like a mongoose after a snake. How, you ask, does he steer with neither hand on the wheel? That's why God gave him knees. You would think that by now the deer would know to run away as soon as they hear a truck revving and a woman screaming….

As the truck swerves toward the fence post, try to not let your mouth freeze open in a silent scream. Brace yourself for the violent turn to the left, away from the fence, just in the nick of time. Thank God, he's finally found the damn binos! But now he's looking through them while driving! Oh crap. He's spotted an elk herd. You might want to assume the crash position: pull your knees up, tuck your head down, and kiss your ass goodbye. He's pounding on buttons to make sure all the windows are down as far as they go, and now he's reaching for the cow calls hanging on lanyards from the rearview mirror. Good, he's selected a call. But why doesn't he pull the lanyard over the mirror? No, instead he leans out of his seat so he can blow on the call while it's still tethered to the mirror. Now his knees can't reach the steering wheel, so the truck is slaloming down the road, back and forth over the double yellow lines. Not that the camo guy notices—he's still gawking through the binos at the elk 300 yards to the left. A few elk look up, glancing our way. Oh yeah! This is the camo guy's reward! His nipples are hard. He shouts, "Twelve—no thirteen, fourteen—cows! Two bulls!" The truck swerves toward the ditch, tires scrabbling at the edge of the pavement. "Ooooooh," the camo guy moans, "one of the bulls is just a spike, but the other is a big guy!" The truck fishtails a little but somehow claws itself back onto the road. "Oh, oh, ohh, ohhhh, what a huge rack! Oh yeah!" If it sounds like a bad porn film, it is, except in this case the actor's lust is real.

The truly amazing thing about this is that the camo guy keeps driving. That's right, he doesn't stop, park the truck, and get out to properly glass the elk. If you ask him, he'll mumble something about not wanting to "spook the herd," but the truth is, he's jonesing to get on down the road to see what other critters he can find. It doesn't matter if that's the biggest bull elk in the county, our camo guy is sure a bigger one is waiting around the next bend. So if you haven't passed out yet from sheer terror, just straighten out your knickers, rub some Vaseline on the seatbelt burns on your neck, and help the poor guy untangle his neck from the lanyards on the rearview mirror before he strangles himself. Whatever you do, don't look at the speedometer, and don't glance back at the carnage of innocent drivers on the road behind you.

YOU EXPECT ME TO POOP
IN THE BUSHES?

Ladies, I realize this is a topic more taboo than talking about sneeze-related bladder leaks. But shit, as they say, happens. Men do it. Boy howdy, do they. And their dogs do it—frequently and in copious amounts if my backyard is anything to go by. Though sometimes I wonder... have you ever noticed how similar man poo and dog poo are? What if that's not all Boomer's business in the yard? Ewwww!

The truth is—cover the children's ears—even those of us among the fairer sex must succumb to the most basic urge now and then. Of course, it's not the fact that we do it that's so mortifying. No, it's that it might cross someone else's mind that we do it, that we are even capable of doing it. Which is why God gave us loud bathroom fans and potpourri in a spray can.

Look at it this way: I've gone to a lot of trouble and no small degree of pain to ensure that my friends, neighbors, and most assuredly any man I've ever dated can be certain beyond a shred of doubt that I do not pass gas. Ever. Not once. Never even a squeak. Fart is not in my vocabulary, so to speak. So hell will freeze solid before anyone ever catches me in the act of actually taking a poop.

This is one of those things that simply should not happen. Thankfully, a civilized society such as ours provides lockable, gender-specific, ventilated, hermetically sealed restrooms with a mysterious and streamlined plumbing system to dispose of the evidence. And when it comes to sneaking in and out of a bathroom unseen, I'm a frickin' ninja.

The problem rears its ugly little head once I leave behind the world of gleaming porcelain bowls and venture into the great outdoors. I have no problem peeing in the bushes if need be, so short outings are fine. But sooner or later, the outdoorsman wants to go camping. That's right—staying out overnight. Sitting around the campfire eating beans and sauerkraut and sloppy joes. Miles from the nearest commode.

I confess. I have tried to hold it in, sometimes for days. I say the Hail Mary prayer of all women in the woods past sunset: "Please let me hold it until I get home!" Sadly, I have to admit this doesn't work. Apparently God's attention to the needs of his supplicants has its limits. Cry, cry, cry....

I am here to tell you that trying to hold it in is doomed to fail and soon becomes a form of self-torture worse than death. I don't care how tight your O-ring is, you cannot hold it in for days. I swear, I have held it so long I could taste it. My back teeth were floating. At some point, your personal plumbing will be full—really, really full, like the Hindenburg just before it exploded and rained fire all over New Jersey—and then there's no stopping it. If you think pooping somewhere out in the bushes is bad, imagine, just as the dam is about to break, not getting out of your sleeping bag fast enough.

Let's face it, you can waddle around crowning like a woman about to give birth for only so long. Sooner or later, that little turtle is going to poke its head out, and then there's no holding back.

But pooping in the bushes is just so gross! I know what you're thinking: "Oh my God, what if someone sees me?" Yes, that is the single most horrifying thought of all. I will walk three miles from camp, setting false tracks and wading creeks like a fugitive, just to make sure that no one follows and no one will see me. But what if the dog tracks me and finds me in my moment of shame? Or what if someone finds the steaming aftermath! Horrifying!

And what if it gets on me? Holy shit! Literally! I would die. I would melt like the wicked witch. How the hell do you squat without putting your feet right in the (ahem) crosshairs? And with your pants down around your ankles—what if it lands in your pants? Even worse, I'm squatting like a sumo wrestler, there in the brambles—hiding in the thickest brush I can find—my bare backside offered like a smorgasbord to a swarm of mosquitoes and horseflies, and I realize two impossibly dire, stomach-churning circumstances: one, the pretty little patch of leaves I've just sat in is poison oak, and two, I'm on more of a slope than I realized. That monster of a brown trout I just released is now rolling toward my shoes!

Few dilemmas in life are so sharply drawn. I cannot sit still and let the rolling, flopping turd land on my shoe. Neither can I leap out of the way—someone might notice the commotion, and who knows what I might land in when I come back down. There's also the small matter of needing to wipe before I move a muscle, or risk giving myself a smelly Rorschach-test butt tattoo.

I'm sorry, but I'm going to leave the outcome of that little scene to your imagination. Allow a woman to preserve some scrap of dignity, won't you? Let's just leave it as a cautionary tale: choose carefully where you squat.

Even in the best-case scenario—okay, there is no such thing as a best scenario when it comes to pooping in the woods—we're still left with the problem of what to do with the doo-doo. The glowing white toilet paper is like a beacon in the night: "Hey-oh, fresh turd over here!" I am pretty sure the miles of toilet paper would be a dead giveaway that a woman left that specific poo pile. How embarrassing! So should I bury it? Should I stir it into the dirt with a stick? Ewww! What am I supposed to do? I don't want anyone to walk by and see it. Or, God forbid, step in it. They'll know that it's mine!

My outdoorsman tells me I'm supposed to bury it, but I don't have a shovel, because, well, you know, I just went for a walk to admire the wildflowers, not to do anything gross. So how am I supposed to dig a hole? I tried using a stick once. It took half an hour to scrape a little divot and then another ten minutes to chase the poo into the hole. I swear, it was like playing pond hockey with pudding for a puck. And I about rubbed the skin right off my hands trying to get them clean; good lord, I touched a stick that was touching poo!

The other option is to dig the hole first, sight in the barrel, aim, and fire away. I tried that. Once. It was the worst game of Pin the Tail on the Donkey I've ever lost. You've seen those laser-guided missiles that pinpoint their target? Well this was more like crop dusting.

So by now you must be wondering, "How does she deal with it?" Here's the scoop. I throw the toilet paper in the bushes a few feet away from the offending turd lying naked on the ground and then I haul ass out of there. Hopefully the toilet paper fluttering around a few feet from the turd will divert the attention of any passersby.

I swear I just do not feel clean after that. I cannot adequately wipe my booty when I am under the pressure of worrying that someone will see. I am all hunkered down in the bushes, frantically trying to poop, wipe, and escape the crime scene before someone walks by. It is so stressful! And how do I wash my hands? Rubbing sanitizer on poopy hands does not feel clean to me! Seriously, I would rather not eat for the entire camping trip than have to poop in the woods. Just thinking about it makes me break a cold sweat.

The outdoorsman loves to poop in the woods. I hear him and his friends talk about it all the time. They get up from the campfire and joke about going "on a bombing run," or "negotiating the release of the hostages." They say they feel one with nature. They shove a roll of toilet paper in their pocket, grab a shovel, and go skipping off into the woods like they're heading to grandma's house for milk and cookies. An hour later they come whistling back into camp without a worry in the world and five pounds lighter. Me, I look like I just committed murder as I frantically scurry back through the bushes, slowing to a saunter as I near camp so no one would dream I've soiled the wilderness.

Years ago, I went camping with a girlfriend and her family. We were out in the woods for two weeks. Her dad, accompanied by four females, took mercy on us and made us a temporary bathroom. It was the most amazing gift I have ever received. How did he make this miracle? He wrapped a tarp around some trees to create a three-walled screen, screwed a board with a hole in it between two stumps, and then placed a toilet seat on the board. He then dug a huge hole and left the dirt and a shovel next to the "toilet." Once you did your duty, you threw a scoop of dirt on the poop, and wah-laaa, it never happened! God love that man. Instant stress-free camp pooping.

Although my girlfriend and I giggled relentlessly as we waited and listened outside the tarp walls while the other one used the facilities, it was wonderful. It was the best camp potty ever.

ROWING LESSONS

Let's go for a float down a lazy river. We'll see ducks and eagles and deer, and we can pull out on a sandy beach in the middle of the river, have a picnic, sunbathe, cool off in the water. Even better, we'll take a raft, so we can carry a cooler full of food and drinks, folding chairs—all the comforts of home! Sounds idyllic, right?

That's the sales pitch I heard, and I bought it hook, line, and sinker. Sure, the camo guy wanted to do some fishing while we were on the river, but it sounded like a fun, relaxing way to spend the day. Then, at the put-in spot on the river, as we were loading everything into the raft, he said the words that changed my life. "I'll give you a quick rowing lesson so I can fish while we float downstream."

I admit, at first, that didn't sound so bad. My camo guy would share his expertise, teaching me a fun skill, and then we'd float away. I looked at the river: it was broad and flat, rippling along at a walking pace. The water was gin clear and about four feet deep. I imagined kicking back in the rowing frame in my bikini, working on my tan while the camo guy caught dinner as we coasted downstream on the current. I mean, it makes sense—the camo guy loves to fish, and that's why he owns the raft. But obviously he can't row the raft and fish at the same time. So I could help out in this small way. Rowing lessons—cool! Suntanning—yay! Cue ominous horror movie music.

When we were ready to launch, the camo guy told

me to sit in the chair attached to the rowing frame. The plastic seat was hot, and some old spilled beer made it sticky, but I made myself at home and grabbed the oar handles, eager to learn. The camo guy pushed the raft into the current, hopped in, and started tying a fly onto his line. While he was busy with that, he gave me the rowing lesson.

"Pull on both oars to go straight, pull on one and push on the other to turn."

"That's it?" I asked.

"Yep. Oh—keep the blades low over the water on the return stroke. And don't splash—it spooks the fish."

By now the raft was spinning slowly into the middle of the river. I pushed down on the oar handles to lift the blades out of the water and swung them backward.

"Keep those out of my casting lanes!" the camo guy barked.

Okay. I let the blades back down into the water and then tugged on the handles. Nothing happened. I tightened my grip and put my back into it. The raft barely nudged forward.

"Take us over to the far bank," the camo guy commanded. "That's where the big trout are."

So I rowed the oars through their sweep again, dipped the blades, and pulled as hard as I could. The raft lumbered downstream, stuck in the middle. I tried again, grunting with the effort.

"C'mon!" he barked again. "We're gonna' miss that deep hole where the lunkers are hiding!"

I dug in again, pulled, raised the blades, dug, pulled, straining at every stroke. Slowly the raft inched across the water. But my forearm muscles were starting to burn, and sweat was trickling down my forehead. I decided to try paddling faster instead of harder, so I swung the oars as quick as I could and dropped them in the water, pulling instantly. But the blades just slapped at the surface.

"No splashing!" the camo guy yelled. "Every trout in the county knows we're here now!"

From my perch up on the rowing frame, I looked at the massive, bright yellow raft floating over the clear water. Where the shadow of the raft broke the glare on the surface, I could see down into the water where dark fish darted back and forth beneath us. The splashing didn't seem to bother these fish. To them, I thought, we must look like the Goodyear blimp blocking the sun. Stealthy. Yeah.

"Wake up!" bellowed the camo guy. "Big bend ahead. Stay out of the eddy!"

I looked up. The river turned right, wrapping around a big gravelly beach, the faster current hugging the outside bank. I scanned the beach but couldn't see anyone, let alone anyone we knew named Eddie.

"Paddle!" the camo guy ordered. "Put us right between the eddy line and the main current!"

"What's an eddy line?" I asked.

The camo guy shot me a look midway between disbelief and aggravation.

"Look over there," he waved toward the beach. "See the smooth water that's not moving?"

"Yeah?"

"That's the eddy, where the river turns back on itself. The seam between the eddy and the main current is the eddy line. That's where the fish are."

I looked at the water. Sure enough, there was an edge where the calm water met the wave-dappled faster current. I dipped the oars and pulled, moving us away from the flat, still water of the eddy. The camo guy whipped his fly line back and forth, the hook buzzing inches from my face, and then dropped the fly on the eddy line. The little dry fly spun at the edge of the current, then twirled into the slack water of the eddy. In a sudden burst, a big, fat trout came from nowhere, gobbled up the fly, and splashed back into the dark water. The camo guy let out a whoop as his line went taut. The reel whined as the big fish ran line off the spool. But the raft was spinning too, away from the fish.

"Bring me around!" the camo guy yelled.

I pulled on the oars, but the raft just slid straight, further into the current.

"No!" he hollered. "Turn! Swing the bow downstream!"

I remembered what he'd said during my "rowing lesson" about pushing one oar and pulling the other, so I tried that. Sure enough, the raft began to rotate. I smiled.

"Not that way!" the camo guy bellowed. He was twisting like a pretzel, trying to keep the tip of his rod pointed downstream toward the fish as the raft swung him the opposite direction. The camo guy spun in a wrestling move to keep his rod aimed at the fish, and just then, the line snapped. The big trout had broken free.

"Aaarrrggghhh!" roared the camo guy. This was followed by rapid-fire, high-decibel cussing. People in a drift boat 300 yards downriver were staring at us. I ducked out of the line of fire by looking down at my sore hands. The palms were red, with blisters starting to form.

That's pretty much how the rest of the morning went—the camo guy issuing commands on precisely where I needed to place the raft, and me rowing as hard as I could, despite my raw hands and aching back. We stopped for lunch at a little island, but there was no beach, just a lot of weeds and biting bugs. Did I mention that I really hate bugs, especially the ones that bite. I ate my sandwich in silence while the camo guy slammed down three beers. He must've noticed how stiff I was as I climbed back into the raft. But instead of taking his turn in the rowing frame, he offered some advice.

"Use your legs when you row, not your back."

I slumped into my seat. More damn rowing lessons, I thought. I was about ready to give him a lesson—a swimming lesson, jerk wad. He pushed the raft away from shore and clambered in. We swung out into the current. I gave a half-hearted tug at the oars, but this time I braced my feet on the metal crossbar spanning the raft and straightened my legs as I pulled. The raft glided over the water, leaving a little wake. I tried it again, and just like that we were in the middle of the river. With renewed energy, I guided the raft around a big rock. The camo guy pointed to the far bank and I rowed right to the spot, then held the raft against the current with a few easy pulls on the oars. He caught a nice little rainbow trout. We meandered on down the river.

Why didn't the camo guy tell me to use my legs from the beginning? Did he expect me to read his mind? I thought about that. Yep, he expected me to read his mind about all sorts of things: where to steer the raft, where he thought the fish were, when to hold over a deep hole, and when to move on. Hell, he probably wanted me to read the fishes' minds to figure out where they were hiding!

I learned my lesson that day all right. No, not the rowing lesson. Instead, I learned that I am not a good mind reader, so it's best if I don't sit in the rowing frame. Sure, I can navigate down the river. I can avoid submerged trees and rocks. I can turn and stop the boat. I can ferry across from one side of the river to the other. But I cannot read the camo guy's mind. Especially when his mind is awash in testosterone and beer, frantic to catch that monster fish. He goes cross-eyed, gets clumsy, tries to do everything all at once, and ends up tangled in his own fly line.

Sound familiar?

I'm happy to report that I've found a solution to all this: fishing lessons.

That's right. I signed up for a women's class at a local fly fishing shop. They taught us how to cast, how to play and land a fish, and how to gently release a fish you don't want to keep. They even taught us how to read the water to know where the fish are hiding. We learned all about dry and wet flies and nymphs. I bought my own rod and reel, and a fishing vest stocked with flies.

Now when the camo guy suggests taking the raft out for a day on the river, I jump right up and start filling the cooler with sandwiches and drinks. I lather up in sunscreen, slide into my sunglasses and vest, and we head for the river. As soon as the boat's on the water, I hop right into the prime fishing seat, no hesitation. You can't hesitate! The guys can sense the slightest indecision on your part and that's when they'll strike, and you'll end up rowing. Just go for it! There's nothing better than a sunny day, clear water full of trout, a wine cooler in a koozie, and a camo guy rowing your raft. Even if you do have to occasionally remind him to keep the oars out of your casting lanes.

EVERYTHING IS AN EMERGENCY

"Holy crap! It's an emergency! I have to go hunting this weekend! It's the only good weekend left."

"Holy crap! It's an emergency! I have to go scouting this weekend because it's already Friday afternoon!"

"Holy crap! It's an emergency! I have to go look for deer at this spot today because it's the only time that they will be there."

"Holy crap! It's an emergency! I have to go across the state of Montana to look for an elk this weekend. I just know that they will be there only this weekend!"

Sound familiar? Yes, everything is an emergency when you are with an outdoorsman. This state of emergency pretty much lasts year-round thanks to all the various hunting seasons. When August rolls around, the emergency is target shooting to get ready for archery season, and then scouting for deer and elk to hunt next month. In September, the emergency is that bow season lasts for only a few weekends so they have to go every weekend. The kicker is, even if they get an animal, then they have to keep going so that all of their buddies get one too. In October, the emergency is that rifle season has begun, and of course they have to blast another elk, deer, pronghorn, or God-knows-what. So of course, every weekend must be devoted to hunting or looking for somewhere to hunt and bugling at every damn thing that moves. November, of course, is the prime hunting time for big bucks because the rut makes the males less wary, more gullible. And not just the human males. No, the bucks get so horny that even a silly man with a piece of plastic hose can easily seduce them by imitating a doe that's ready to mate. The buck comes running when he hears the call, and then the hunter blasts him! That just seems beyond cruel to me, using the male's own hormones to lure him in and then blammo! Then again, if you toned it down a notch, it might be just the ticket for getting your man to finally tackle the household chores he always sneaks out of. Hmmmmm…(note to self).

The calendar turns to December and we're thinking holidays and family get-togethers, but of course that's turkey season. No, not roast turkey and stuffing. We're talking blasting away at big toms with a 12-gauge shotgun. So if you were hoping to relax to some Christmas songs, you'll have to use headphones to hear anything over the endless turkey gobbling and scratching calls. By this point I'm agreeing with my outdoorsman—yes, it is an emergency because I'm having a massive stroke from all the obnoxious turkey call practicing!

Just when you think you can't take any more, January arrives, kicking off the good duck and goose season, with more honking and quacking on every road trip and anytime a bird hunting video is on the television. We're also into ice fishing now, which makes every day an emergency because the fish are biting! And the ice might thaw tomorrow! February brings the "late" mountain lion season. If you didn't go cat hunting in December, you get a second "emergency" chance! Somehow the outdoorsman cannot remember our anniversary in February, but he's always ready on opening day for the big cats. March is the final emergency for ice fishing and the onslaught of boat shows. April brings the spring turkey season, because we need to shoot all the turkeys that survived the earlier season! Cue more gobbling and screeching. April also kicks off horn hunting and full-on tick season. No, we don't hunt ticks—they hunt us! May is an emergency because the spring black bear season ends and he's still loaded for bear. Holy crap! May also launches the fishing season—a whole new emergency!—but the best spring creek runs are in June. July is hatch time—pale dun, salmonfly, caddis—each one a major emergency: the hatch is on! Which brings us round again to August.

Living with an outdoorsman, every weekend is an emergency. Every damn weekend is the peak of the rut or hatch or migration. They have to go today because tomorrow might be too late! Of course, they never know if the animals will in fact be where they expect them to be, so the emergency might get bumped to the following weekend, which has its own hunting or fishing crisis, and then heads spin because you have a double emergency!

God forbid they miss a chance at that one big buck because they were sleeping in and making French toast with their woman on a lazy Saturday morning, or God forbid they not limit out on their duck and goose license because they took their kids sledding instead. Why are family things always an afterthought? Oh sure, the outdoorsman pretends to be interested, casually asking what the plans are for the weekend. But really he's asking, "When can I squeeze in my hunting without getting axe-murdered by my pissed-off, sick-of-being-alone wife?"

I've come to grips with the fact that my outdoorsman is always on the go, that he "needs" to hunt and fish. I knew this when I married him, and I don't expect him to change…much. But I still reserve the right to kick his bugling, honking, quacking, mewing, howling ass once in a while to remind him that, from where I stand, it's open season on his hide year-round, any time, any day.

ALWAYS PREPARED

MacGyver has nothing on my camo guy. Sure, MacGyver may be able to make a life raft out of a rubber band and a Q-tip, but my camo guy is always prepared for any situation. He doesn't need rubber bands or Q-tips to make his life raft because he'll have the actual damn life raft. With a first-aid kit. And Sterno and storm-proof matches. And canned beans. Lots of canned beans.

What some people see as clutter, my camo guy calls the bare necessities. Take a look inside the stink wagon. Wait! Oops, I didn't mean actually opening the door to look inside! Now we'll have to pick up all the crap that fell out and cram it back in there. Yep, the truck is packed to the gills with "essential" stuff. You name it and it's in that truck. There are four pairs of boots, several sets of gloves (if you don't mind that none of them match), six pairs of sunglasses, two rolls of duct tape, a dog bed, three wool army blankets, a large bag of sunflower seeds, a really large bag of soggy sunflower seed hulls, a rusty hatchet, enough CDs to shingle the Luxor pyramid in Las Vegas, zip ties scattered everywhere, several quarts of engine oil, a box of Kleenex, an old tractor inner tube (partially inflated), assorted cargo straps and bungee cords, a roll of plastic garbage bags, a poker deck of playing cards, ten no-spill coffee mugs (but only three lids), a bag of petrified elk jerky, at least one tennis ball under each seat, pieces of fishing rods, a half-open tackle box with lures and knots of line spilling out, an old folding knife, a Swiss

Army knife, a multi-tool, a large sheath knife without the sheath, and a machete. And that's just the front seat.

MacGyver himself could probably build a Mars rover just with the stuff hanging from the rearview mirror. Duck calls, goose calls, an elk bugle, sunglasses, a chainsaw chain, dog tags, a St. Hubert medal, and too many fishing lures to count. I'm sure there are enough chemicals in the flock of air fresheners to fuel the Mars rover for decades. (Honestly, I should give up on the air fresheners. There is nothing more obnoxious than the stink of stale farts, wet dog, and rotten food mingling with strawberry delights, cinnamon swirls, and lavender fields.)

The jockey box is so full of crap that it won't latch. Random keys, foam ear plugs, a roll of electrical tape, a greasy bandanna, an even greasier banana, a wooden clothespin, a bottle of ibuprofen, ear buds, measuring tape, a broken rifle bore brush, and a set of rubber buck teeth. Yeah, you read that right—costume fake teeth. So when you run out of ammo, you can smile and the deer will die laughing.

Of course there's the usual assortment of screwdrivers, pliers, socket wrenches, hose clamps, and broken air pressure gauges. Along with a whole catalog of bows, target arrows, hunting arrows, loose bow strings, releases (at least one of each: wrist, t-grip trigger, finger caliper), camo arm guards, spare arrow nocks, a foam target block, and nasty broadhead arrow points floating around in the seat cushions. Never mind the half-empty boxes of rifle cartridges, shotgun shells, and .22 rounds. Oh, and shooting glasses, a day-glo orange vest, and three sets of "tactical" earmuffs. A blowgun. (Wait, really? What, are we moving to the Amazon?) And more than enough handguns, rifles, and shotguns to survive the zombie apocalypse or World War III, whichever comes first.

That's the cab. I don't even want to know what's in the back of the truck.

I hate riding in the stink wagon, mostly because of the smell, but all the clutter makes it even more uncomfortable. Finding a place to sit is like trying to shovel out from an avalanche while the snow is still sliding down the mountain. No matter how fast you dig, the opening fills back in before you can see the bottom. If you do manage to clear a spot, you'll still end up with a dry fly snagged in your backside or a loose rifle cartridge working its way into your yoga pants like a slow-motion heat-seeking missile. Then, when the truck lurches into motion, all that crap starts bouncing around the cab like ice cubes in a blender. As bad as it is dodging fishing reels and flying tire irons, a ricocheting tree stand is the worst—those suckers have more sharp corners than Madonna's bra.

As much as I hate to admit it, all of this clutter comes in handy. Given the sorts of accidental adventures we get into, it's nice to know we're riding in a half-ton survival kit. Need a gauze bandage? Last week's T-shirt will do, and it's right there in the backseat. Hungry? A whole football team could live for a week foraging on the M&Ms, raisins, and free-range peanuts hiding in the upholstery. Forgot the tent? Here, unfold this tarp while I string a ridgeline made from bootlaces. We can stake out the corners with these coat hangers.

There's always a flashlight when you need one, even if you have to rummage around for the batteries. And rummaging keeps you warm, especially stink-wagon rummaging, which is an endurance sport. Finding what you need in the bowels of the stink wagon is an extreme triathlon of digging, powerlifting, and tug-of-war. But no matter what you need, the prize is always there. Food, water, clothing, shelter—the stink wagon provides. The last time we went camping, I asked my camo guy to build a campfire. He ran to the truck and came back with kitchen matches, a lighter, and a propane torch. He pulled kindling and a few branches out of the back, then spent twenty minutes deciding which "fire starter" to use—Sterno in a tin, a bottle of white gas, a jug of diesel fuel, or a can of kerosene.

If their trucks are anything to go by, every camo guy is similarly well provisioned. They all hoard stuff because "you never know when you might need it." And most of them are really good at "re-purposing" whatever is at hand in response to the crisis of the moment. They get really creative on trips into the backcountry—I've seen a paper clip jury-rigged into a fish hook and the margins torn off a topo map to serve as toilet paper. Once, on a late fall hunting trip, the camo guy forgot his little cookstove. It was cold and we were hungry; I was looking forward to a hot bowl of freeze-dried stew. After emptying everything from his pack and still no stove, he sat down and drank a beer. I thought, "Oh great, no hot food tonight." Then he pulled out a pocketknife, unfolded the blade, belched, and stabbed the empty beer can. I thought, "Oh great, now he's drunk and angry." But in no time he'd fashioned that can into a little woodburning stove. He fed twigs into the firebox and boiled a pot of water in less than five minutes.

It would've been perfect if he'd remembered to pack the food.

HOT DATE

hat you're about to read sounds like one of those redneck jokes, but I can assure you, this is no laughing matter. You know you're dating an outdoorsman…if you've ever been on a hot date that featured tearing live worms in half. Or if the date's "special dinner" was corn dogs from a gas station. Or if the beer was warm and your feet, hands, and nose were cold. You sure as hell are dating an outdoorsman if the "romance" includes a corsage of prickly weeds clinging to your clothes, dancing the two-step waiting in line at a pit toilet outhouse, and long, passionate, wet kisses…from his Labrador retriever.

An outdoorsman's sense of romance never wanders too far from his peculiar sense of fun. Which means your first date will likely involve bouncing down a bone-jarring jeep track in a filthy truck, hiking through a swamp in the rain, close inspection of an old elk carcass, shooting cans off a fence rail, and shaking from near-hypothermia in the dark while you look for the truck, which the intrepid outdoorsman is sure awaits just over the next ridge.

Now don't be shocked or insulted by these unique date activities. They're simply his idea of true romance. Don't hold your breath for store-bought flowers, a fancy dinner, or a chick flick. Those aren't on an outdoorsman's radar. He would much rather show you what a real man he is by demonstrating his primal qualities and skills. You know, like throwing rocks, climbing trees, spearing fish, making animal noises, and generally pounding his hairy chest. All of these activities are designed to make your inner cave woman swoon over what a great mate and provider he will be. If during the date he happens to grunt, simply return the compliment and grunt back. He will smile, and you should be grateful for his interest in conversation. Choose your words carefully, however—too much grunting on your part may encourage even more primal behavior on his part.

After a number of these dates, I learned to bring a bag filled with spare clothes for any occasion, soap, shampoo, extra shoes, deodorant, and some makeup. After a day of fishing, hiking, carcass skinning, and muddy dog wrestling, you'll want to be prepared for suddenly arriving back in civilization. On a whim, you may end up at a steak house or a hokey action-adventure movie, sitting next to people who may not share your newfound enthusiasm for dead fish, swamp muck, and wet dogs.

Look on the bright side: when you date an outdoorsman, you will never be bored, never stiff from sitting still too long, and never wishing for a little comedy in your life. At the very least, you will be introduced to outdoor activities that you never knew existed, you'll meet animals that you had no idea were edible, and you'll be endlessly entertained by the bewildering, testosterone-fueled antics of your intrepid outdoorsman. It really is not so bad, particularly if he has his shirt off....

CAMOUFLAGE LINGERIE

Let's be clear about one thing—the point of putting on lingerie is to feel sexy. I want to feel alluring and desirable, and I want my man to notice. Maybe even get him revved up a bit. I like lace, I like satin, and I like sexy colors. Risqué colors—glossy black, racy red, or hot pink. Something frisky to catch my man's eye.

Apparently I've been doing it all wrong. If the gifts I receive from the outdoorsman are any indication, he'd rather I was invisible. Yep, that's right. He buys me camouflage camisoles, bark-patterned panties, bras that blend into upland bird hunting habitat.

How does this work, exactly? He thinks me looking like a tree is sexy? The thought of my body covered in bark does it for him? What the hell? Does he walk around in the woods turned on all the time by tree bark and random shrubs?

Oh yeah, I can see it now. I have my Mossy Oak® camouflage bra and panties on, lounging seductively on the Mossy Oak® camouflage comforter on our bed. I wonder, if there was a mirror on the ceiling, would my naughty bits be invisible? Would I look like a magician's saw-the-girl-in-half act gone horribly wrong?

There's nothing like a babydoll printed in leaves and branches to make a girl feel so…earthy. What the hell! Sorry, but "earthy" isn't the mood I'm looking for when it comes to seducing my man. What, should I just forget about waxing or shaving and go "natural?" I could skip bathing, too. Yeah, then he'd come to bed and I'd be waiting there, hidden by all the leaves, branches, and grass, lying in wait like a hairy, smelly Sasquatch. Oh yeah! Please baby, baby, please buy me some camouflage undies so I can unleash my inner yeti on you!

And here's another thing. Would somebody please explain pink camo lingerie to me? It's standard camo—a jigsaw puzzle of leaves and bark—but it's pink! I don't get it. Under what possible scenario does bubblegum pink camouflage make sense? An armed invasion of camo Barbie dolls? Sigh…I suppose I'll take any gift I can get.

You might be able to persuade me that seeing his woman in camouflage lingerie makes a man feel primal and savage. But if he wants to go all Neanderthal in the bedroom, why am I wearing a sheer polyester camo teddy? Shouldn't I be wrapped in furs? Shouldn't he be handing me a mastodon leg to gnaw on? And he'd be strutting around in nothing but a skimpy loincloth, right? Now we're talking.

OUTDOORSMAN GIFTS

As Camo Queens, we women deserve to be regaled with compliments, praise, and gifts. Especially gifts. Unfortunately, by the very nature of our relationships with outdoorsmen, these gifts are likely to be more "interesting" than the average box of chocolates.

In the old days, a cave man would bring home pretty pebbles, a fur hide, or some berries. I'm guessing the woman looked at these trinkets about the same way I view the mouse heads my cat leaves on our doorstep. Actually, I'm not guessing at all, because to this day I do in fact receive pebbles, squirrel tails, entire dead fish, animal teeth, horns, dead ducks, slabs of random (and unidentifiable) raw meat, styrofoam coffee cups full of worms, pieces of tree bark, and turkey feathers as gifts. On a weekly basis. Yes, I am serious. If these things appeared on my doorstep, I'd know that my cat was showing its appreciation. But these "gifts" are usually left on the dining room table, or on my nightstand. That's my guy.

Does this show his love for me? Does this mean he thinks that I have a nice set of teeth, good birthing hips, and he hopes I will pick him to be my mate? What the hell are you supposed to do with this stuff? My queenly manners tell me that I must smile and reward the outdoorsman with a kiss and hug. My girly instincts want to use a long-handled shovel to fling the "prize" into the bushes and then run away.

I have learned, through personal trauma, that if the outdoorsman hands you a bag that you cannot see into, you should be afraid. Very, very afraid. Girls with a ticklish gag reflex might want to think twice before getting involved with a guy who wears camo.

Of course, the unevolved outdoorsman does also occasionally purchase some gifts. You know, for special occasions like your birthday or Christmas. Diamond earrings? Spa gift certificates? Fabulous perfume? Oh hell no! I am talking bow and arrows, assorted guns, raccoon-skin hats, hiking boots, fishing poles, and rounds of ammo. Sigh. . . .

I realize that the outdoorsman thinks these are the absolute best gifts ever because these are what he would want. I do have to give him credit for trying...he does buy them all in pink. And I know that you know what I'm talking about, because now you can find pink camo plastered on everything from assault rifles to bustiers and bikini bottoms.

I love the fact that getting a gift from an outdoorsman is really always a surprise. Sure, this surprise might scare the ever-living crap out of you—some of the gifts are still capable of biting! But I can guarantee that you'll never be able to guess what sort of gift you will receive. While other women are forced to feign joy over yet another slinky black dress or diamond pendant, the Camo Queen savors genuine astonishment. Nothing spells L-O-V-E to the outdoorsman like surprising his mate with a sexy, hot pink rifle sling or a gas-powered ice-fishing auger. I can sense how jealous you all must be.

THE ROMANCE OF CAMPING

Camping makes for fond memories—fresh air, blue skies, evenings around a campfire, roasting marshmallows, noshing on s'mores, snuggling into a warm sleeping bag and being lulled to sleep by the scent of balsam and the soft hoot of a distant owl.

I will never forget a particular camping trip I went on with the outdoorsman and my then-teenage brother. Our simple agenda was to have fun, indulge in a little fishing, but mainly just float this particular river and camp out on an island. Our first day on the river was a scorcher— no relief from the sun and soaring temperatures. Teenage boys are stinky anyway, but broil one in the sun for a few hours and the needle on the rank-o-meter is pegged at "lethal." Even my outdoorsman was quite ripe from rowing a raft all day in the August heat. Men who smell bad—imagine that.

We get to our island and my outdoorsman sets up camp, starting with a "two-man" tent. I'm reminded of that old joke: "How many people can sleep in a two-man tent?" If you think the obvious answer is "two," then you've clearly never crawled inside one of these diaper-sized nylon traps. (That's not a typo—properly set up, a tarp would be a palace compared to this stinkhole tent.) My outdoorsman is oblivious to all this even as he squeezes his shoulders into the tent, cooing "Home sweet home!" I can see his elbows bulging both sides of the tent out, and his head makes a bump in the ceiling. His legs dangle out the door. With a grunt, he rolls onto his side and the whole tent twists with the motion. "I didn't know Coleman made straightjackets," I say. "Good thing there are only three of us." Let the fun really begin.

Just to be clear, I don't think it's in the least sexist to call this marvel of compaction a two-man tent. No self-respecting woman should ever poke even the tip of her nose inside one of these things.

Evening rolls on and we cook up a trout on the fire. Everyone is merry, drinking beer licking fish grease off their fingers, and life is good until the first crack of thunder. Lightning dances overhead, followed by a biblical downpour. So all three of us rapidly wriggle into the tent like larvae in a cocoon to get pretty dang cozy. Boy howdy that tent is muggy. Instantly it's a sweat lodge perfumed with eau de raw onions, armpits, funky cheese, and of course loud, rippling man farts. The only difference between the rumbling inside the tent and outside from the storm is that thunder doesn't produce waves of pure stank.

The air inside that tent is so thick you can see it. Oh my God. We are going to be stuck in here for hours to come. Help! Please make the rain stop! It's not like you ever get true-blue sleep in a tent anyways, but this is out of control. Holy steaming dog crap! By now, my gag reflex is on a hair trigger. I glance at my watch—2 a.m. Sweet Jesus. I roll over and my face lands one inch from my brother's face, which is one inch from the snoring outdoorsman's hairy, rotten armpit. My brother's eyes are watering from the tear gas. He blinks and whispers, "I can't breathe! If I don't get some fresh air, I'm gonna die!" In heartfelt sympathy, I start giggling. Then full-out snorting and laughing. "It's NOT funny!" wails my brother. Now I'm howling. The outdoorsman, predictably, sleeps through this like a baby. A big, bloated, farting baby.

The rain comes down harder and the ceiling of the tent is dripping, though I'm guessing it's just condensation from all the farts. But the "waterproof" floor is flooding now—which means once the water gets in, it puddles and pools like a lagoon at high tide. So I elbow the outdoorsman in the kidneys and hint that his woman is displeased. He grunts, sits up, and says, with a look of complete innocence, "What's the matter?"

That's it. I slither out of the A-frame cesspool and gasp fresh air in the pouring rain. My brother stumbles out, retching a little. The rain is cold, but I'm just hoping it will rinse off the smell. My brother shivers and says, "I'm not going back in there." Just then, the outdoorsman sticks his head out of the tent and says, "There's a big tarp in the raft. We can rig a shelter out of that."

So at 2:30 a.m. we claw our way around in the dark, lining a rope between two trees and pulling the tarp over it for a rough lean-to. We are finally out of the rain and breathing fresh air. Praise the lord!

Which is when the spiders and mosquitoes find us. Apparently spiders don't want to get wet either, so they start crawling all over us. Not just one or two, but dozens of the prickly little biters. Grossss! All of this sheer fun, along with mosquitoes the size of hummingbirds buzzing in my ears, nose, and mouth. Is this friggin' Borneo? I tell ya, when I finally woke up the next morning, I had mosquito and spider bites everywhere. Yes, even there! Did I forget to mention that the only bathroom on this island resort was a squat in the bushes? There is nothing quite like getting poked in the unsuspecting butt cheek by a sharp stick or tickly grass as you squat down in the bushes to relieve yourself. And as if it's not bad enough to get speared, you usually get at least a couple of mosquito bites right on the cheeks. Nothing like spending the rest of the evening scratching your booty!

As I write this I am laughing at the memory. How can life get better than that? You know, the most miserable outings make for the best stories. Now, every time I drive by that stretch of river, I start laughing. The things we do to make our outdoorsmen happy. . . .

TOOTHBRUSHES? SHOWERS? NOT SHAVING? OH, MY!

Who needs clean teeth? A shower? A shave? The outdoorsman can survive forever without these simple pleasures. He can go a whole weekend without touching a bar of soap. I've seen him disappear into the woods for weeks at a time without a toothbrush. Seriously, three weeks without brushing his teeth. Oh! My! God! Talk about a petri dish full of wriggling germs. Can you imagine the disease growing on those pearly whites? Not to mention how his breath smells? It's bad enough that he doesn't brush, but he's also eating nonstop hot dogs, beans, stale cheese, and warm beer. He came home from a long hunting trip one time and tried to kiss me at the front door. I threw up in my mouth a little, and that was just from his breezy "Hi babe!" I swear, it smelled like the time the dog knocked over the neighbor's trash can and rolled in the dirty diaper.

How can these outdoorsmen not be bothered by their own stink? After one of his adventures, my guy's pits are worse than raw onions, and his breath peels the paint right off the ceiling. Then he kicks his boots off. I don't know if I can describe that…my stomach starts to churn just thinking about it. His feet unleash the tang of burning rubber, a dash of rotten eggs, and the zest of toenail fungus. Bloated dead things don't smell that bad. I don't understand the chemical reaction that occurs when you place clean feet into freshly laundered socks and then slip them into hunting boots. Granted, they stew in those boots for days on end, all sweaty and oily. But where do the toxic fumes come from? How do the microbial, sulfurous spawn from Hell get into those boots?

Don't get me started on his undies. He won't change them for the entire trip. Really? How much weight would it add to his pack to carry even just one fresh pair? But no, he comes home after a week in the woods and tosses his stanky clothes in the laundry pile, and from the looks of those undies, I'm guessing he has to use an industrial belt sander to peel them off. The first time I ever did his laundry after a long hunting trip, I found skid marks that would make any brodie-spinning teenager proud. I now use a pair of old barbecue tongs to load the washing machine.

We now have a rule: When he gets home from a hunting trip, he keeps those oniony armpits, rotten teeth, and revolting feet away from me until they are all cleaned up. And if he slathers himself in wild animal urine or estrus cologne, he can just forget it—he's not coming near me until he sheds his skin. I'm not cuddling with a guy who smells like some old cow's naughty bits! I love my outdoorsman, but there are limits.

I never have understood how in the heck the outdoorsman lives with himself smelling like a rotting corpse. Or why he would think anyone else would put up with his rank stank. They may call it "personal" hygiene, but really we stay clean for social reasons, right? I mean, if no one else can stand the smell of you, chances are you're not going to have many "close" friends. People tend to avoid things that trigger their gag reflexes.

Which makes it that much weirder when the outdoorsman and I go roughing it for several days in the backcountry, and there's no chance to bathe or even freshen up a little, so we're both getting ripe, and he still wants to get frisky. Really? I can live with my own sour perfume for a few days, but only if no one else comes sniffing too close. Yet here comes the outdoorsman, hot to trot. Being filthy and smelly makes me feel many things, but sexy is not one of them. The thought of jumping in the sack together makes me shiver in anticipation—but not in a sexy way. Dread? Yes. Desire? Not so much.

Seriously, my breath is curling my own nose hairs, and my armpits feel greasy. I have hairs sprouting like spider legs from my bikini line, and the highway patrol could use the stubble on my legs as spike strips to stop a fugitive's car. Even if I could put all this out of my mind for a few moments of passion, I'd worry that my man would be scarred for life. He'd never look at me the same.

Bottom line: if there is to be nookie, there will first be showers, toothbrushes, and shaving cream. No exceptions.

Not that a shower is always the best answer. I remember one early November hunting trip when we'd been camping for three days—a full twenty-four hours beyond my usual limit for going without a shower—and I was desperate to de-grease and de-stink. We were tent camping—no cozy RV or fifth-wheel with a shower for us, no sir. But the outdoorsman assured me I could clean up right there in the campground. So he opened a door on the truck, draped the filthy, hairy, muddy dog blanket over the door, and told me to undress and stand behind the door. I was sure the neighbors would be able to see me, but I really wanted to lather up and get clean. I figured if I was quick and quiet about it, maybe no one would notice. So I stripped down—damn, it's cold, and there's a sharp breeze—and the outdoorsman handed me an old bar of soap. I say "old," but what I really mean is ancient, like a relic unearthed from an archaeological dig. The soap was small and gray, with lots of embedded hairs and specks of dirt. I was about to complain that there had to be a better bar of soap when the heavens opened up and a torrent of ice water hit my head and naked body. Lordy, cold doesn't begin to describe it. I screamed, and the outdoorsman laughed, standing there with an empty five-gallon bucket.

"Well what are you waiting for, suds up!" he said.

"W-w-w-w-where d-d-d-d-did you f-f-f-f-find the w-w-w-w-water?" I chattered.

"The pump is shut off for winter," he said, "so I filled the bucket down at the creek."

The creek? The creek that had ice along its banks this morning? I wanted to scream again, but my skin had turned blue and rigor mortis was setting in, so I started frantically scrubbing with the scrap of dirty soap. I lathered up my face and my hair, and then, blinking through the suds, worked my way all the way down to my feet, shivering like a cellphone set to vibrate. Brrrrrrrrrr! Then the rinse water hit and I went from cold to flash-frozen. But strangely enough, as my shivering went to full-on shaking, I could hear the high whistle of a steam kettle at full boil. The sound seemed to be coming from far away, and I clung to it as some small vestige of warmth in a world gone suddenly arctic, until I realized that it was my own shrieking.

So much for trying to be sneaky. At this point, I didn't really care who was gawking at me, all I wanted to do was dry off, pile on warm clothes, and drink a gallon of scalding hot chocolate. The outdoorsman, always prepared, handed me a towel, and I went into a frenzy of rubbing my face, my hair, my whole body, grateful for the friction and shelter from the breeze. Until I noticed a smell, a truly wicked odor. And my skin thawed enough to register a harsh, scratchy sensation. I stopped rubbing and looked at my towel. Sure enough, it wasn't a towel at all but the filthy, hairy, muddy dog blanket that had been covering the window in the door. Not only did I smell worse than I had before the "shower," but I was giving quite a show to half a dozen hunters in the adjacent campsite. Who were all looking my way, swaddled in wool pants and down coats, standing with their backs to a roaring fire, smiling and sipping from steaming mugs.

I quickly got dressed—at least the fresh clothes were clean—did some jumping jacks to get the blood flowing again, and grabbed a comb. I'd never washed my hair with soap before. It didn't feel right, and it felt even worse when I tried to comb it. Between the soap and overzealous rubbing to dry off, I had created the world's biggest tumbleweed on my head. My hair looked like it was housing a pack rat. Or a family of pack rats. And that's how it stayed for two more days, too painful to comb out. I would've given my left ovary for a dab of conditioner.

After all that, the outdoorsman kissed me on the cheek and told me how cute I was. I hit him.

TRUCK LUST

Being an outdoorsman apparently keeps a man young at heart. Even in his thirties, my guy still has the mind of a hormone-riddled, combustion-motor-obsessed, sixteen-year-old boy. Sometimes his voice cracks into a high-pitched screech when he screams in ecstasy as we drive by one of the three truck dealerships in our town. At least once a month we cruise through the dealership parking lots to inspect the new trucks, the old trucks, and the plain ol' badass trucks. I scoot as far down in my seat as I can, praying that none of the slimy salesmen will make it out to our truck before the outdoorsman is done drooling over the truck selection. If one of the greaseballs does waddle out fast enough, I can guarantee that I'll be hearing that same sales pitch at the dinner table for at least two weeks.

Just when you think the outdoorsman has forgotten about the newest, baddest, loudest, sweetest, biggest, diesel smokin' truck that gets great gas mileage, the sales pitch begins again. It never fails—after every hunting trip with his fellow gnarly, tire-burnout-obsessed buddies, he comes home "needing" a new truck. This is despite the fact that his truck is only one year old and just last year it was the coolest thing he had ever seen and had more selling points than even a used car salesman could come up with. Now the same truck is a dog. I hear the litany of faults: terrible gas mileage, unsafe to ride in, not enough room, the engine makes funny noises, the brakes are failing, the shocks are shot, and the upholstery is too girly. The list goes on and on. This year, leather seats are in and fabric is old school. This year, diesel is to die for and only a fool would still be driving a regular gas engine. This year, the new Ford is the business and last year's Ford is suddenly a bad joke.

It blows my mind that such a complete transformation can occur in twelve months or less. Sure, the outdoorsman beats the ever-loving shit out of his truck on a daily basis. He uses it on rough mountain roads, fording creeks, grinding over boulders and downed trees, and hauling big-ass dead animals. But that's why he gets the heavy-duty, high-clearance model, right? Besides, what's the point of bragging about having an engine that will last for 300,000 miles if you trade it in after only 30,000 miles? Why worry about new leather seats when you can't even see the old upholstery for all the dog and deer hair?

I do have to give him one thing—his year-old truck no longer has that "new car" smell. Boy howdy. Let's be honest here. An out-doorsman's new truck goes from sweet to sour in about three days. Or less than a day if he buys the truck during hunting season. You can't haul dogs and dead meat and expect that fresh-off-the-lot smell to linger.

So if you have an outdoorsman in your life, there's no way around it. You just have to budget for a new rig every year. The good news is that unlike people who hold onto their vehicles for decades, you never spend money replacing tires, windshields, wiper blades, or oil filters. Heck, he probably won't own the rig long enough to bother changing the oil. And as filthy and stinky as that truck will get, even at its worst, it's only one year's worth of filth and stink. Be thankful for small blessings.

THE BIBLE

Does your outdoorsman pray every single day? Does he worship the Bible diligently? Does he know the Bible word for word? Does his Bible sit on the back of the toilet? Does his Bible have a mule deer buck on the front?

I remember the first time my outdoorsman saw the hardback edition of the Cabela's catalog. We were at my dad's house for dinner. My dad had received a copy of the catalog in the mail and had left it sitting on the kitchen counter. My guy wasn't even done shaking hands when he zeroed in on the catalog. A look of pure rapture came over his face as his eyes traced the path of light straight from heaven down to the cover. The outdoorsman's breathing became shallow and fast, his cheeks turned rosy, and his eyes teared up a little as he lovingly caressed the cover.

He immediately wanted to know how he too might receive such a holy text. My dad did not know why he was one of the chosen few, but he thought maybe it was because he had a Cabela's credit card and spent a certain amount of money there each year. "A certain amount of money" apparently is outdoorsman code for "take out a second mortgage on your home." Dad hadn't finished this thought before the outdoorsman was applying for the credit card with his smartphone.

All through dinner, the outdoorsman had a moon-struck, hormone-infused look on his face. It's the look he gets when we're alone and he's in the mood. So I discreetly stroked his ankle with my toe under the table. He nearly jumped out of his chair, glanced at me, and then turned his gaze back to the catalog. I realized it wasn't me he wanted to ravage.

When my dad was done with that catalog, he gave it to the outdoorsman. I'm pretty sure we still have that original First Testament on our bookshelf. The outdoorsman loved and caressed that book for years. Then, one day—known in our household as the Second Coming—the mailman made a special delivery. June 3, 2009. A Wednesday. The parcel weighed three pounds, six ounces and measured nine by twelve inches. It was waiting for him when the outdoorsman came home from work. He wept. From that day on, the Cabela's hardback was called the "Bible."

Not a night goes by without the Bible being read. Not a poop session occurs empty-handed, and never are they less than forty-five minutes long thanks to his reading of the gospel. He has a small altar on the coffee table in our living room—a stack of Bibles from previous years.

I'm careful to watch for the mailman when the next Bible is due. On the day it arrives, I take a photo of it with my phone and send it to the outdoorsman. Then I hide the Bible where I know it will never be found. When the outdoorsman arrives home from work he is frantic. He hollers, "Where is it?" He grovels and begs. I stand my ground, for in that moment, I can have anything I want.

Do I want another baby? A puppy of my own? A diamond ring? Or a three-hour, all-too-rare frisky massage? More often, I wait until he's despondent, tearfully pleading with me, and then remind him of a household project he's been procrastinating on. (And by procrastinating, I mean three years ago he agreed to do it and hasn't lifted a tool since.) I tell you what, that project will be completed faster than I can say "please." While he's busy, I sneakily retrieve the hidden Bible and leave it under a magazine on the kitchen counter. I also grab his credit cards. Then, when the project is done, I tell him to look under the magazine. I walk to the door and listen to his heavy breathing and "oh baby!" moans as he flips through the first pages. And then I go shopping. He won't even know I'm gone for at least six hours.

Sure, it's a little weird that he gets hot and bothered over a shopping catalog. At first, it stung a bit. I was jealous. But then I realized what a godsend it is. When he gets lost in the book, it keeps him out of my hair for hours. And if he wants to get frisky when I'm not in the mood, the Bible is the perfect decoy. All I have to do is casually open the cover—it doesn't matter what page falls open—and he swoons. Maybe I've learned a few things from hanging around my outdoorsman. He's not the only one who knows how to lure in a horny critter during the rut. . . .

WHEN IN DOUBT, BLAST IT

Have you ever noticed how outdoorsmen always carry an arsenal of weapons in their trucks, ready for WWIII? Some of them are sneaky and keep the big guns hidden under the seat, while others show them off in charming gun racks that fill the back windows of their trucks. But a quick inventory of any outdoorsman's rig reveals rifles, shotguns, handguns, knives, hatchets, pocketknives, slingshots, and at least one "tactical" flashlight designed to bash skulls in (while keeping the bulb intact so you can shine a light on the bloody mess you've made).

My outdoorsman mostly hunts deer and elk, so why does he need a gun designed to bring down elephants? Why does he need a sniper rifle that can pick a gnat off a weasel's rear end at 1,000 yards? And why does he need so many damn guns at all? What the heck does he think is going to charge him—a Sasquatch in a Kevlar vest? Ten rabid grizzly bears? Why on earth does the truck need to be in a constant state of readiness for the apocalypse?

I feel bad for anyone who decides to mess with an outdoorsman. Honestly, they will get blasted seven different ways, stabbed, suffocated, bonked, and spit on. If the poor sap manages to escape, it will not be for long. The outdoorsman will simply launch one of his drones and nuke the fugitive with a laser-guided bunker buster. If the missile doesn't get him, one of the outdoorsman's dogs will. No, the dog won't kill him. But the dog will hold the guy until the outdoorsman saunters up. Clearly, anyone who would mess with an outdoorsman doesn't know the cardinal outdoorsman rule: when in doubt, blast it!

This applies to anything, anywhere. See, similar to most birds, outdoorsmen undergo a molt, generally toward the end of summer. They gradually shed their fishing gear and sprout their fall plumage, which consists of camo and lots and lots of firearms and knives. Their demeanor changes, too, from patient angler to pent-up, testosterone-fueled, blood-lusting hunter. Once they taste the hunting frenzy, you'll want to stay out of the woods. The second that the calendar indicates that it is indeed hunting season, their eyes cross, their trigger fingers start to twitch, they douse themselves in wild animal piss, and they sneak around in the woods jacked up on endless pots of coffee.

Suddenly, everything is a target. A tree branch creaking under the weight of snow? Blast it! A squirrel jumping away from the tree? Blast it! The pinecone dropped by the now-defunct squirrel? Blast it? I tell you, nothing's safe. A coyote running across the prairie, a snake slithering across the road, a gopher poking his head out of a hole in the dirt—it's open season! Blast away! Soda cans, highway signs, old hubcaps in the ditch—fill 'em with lead!

Now I know someone's going to read this and say, "A few crazies give hunters a bad name—most people are responsible gun owners." And they're probably right. So the moral of this little story is: when you see a deer-crossing sign blasted full of bullet holes, drive faster—there's a crazy person on the loose, he has a gun, and your hubcaps might be next.

IS MY BOOTY FROZEN OFF?

Remember, fellow Camo Queens, the good old days when you first met your outdoorsman and you were willing to do all sorts of "new" things just to be able to hang out with him? God forbid you'd be away from each other for half a day! I remember the first time my camo guy conned me into duck hunting in the middle of winter because all his hunting buddies were busy. He made it sound like fun: we would snuggle on a bench in a sheltered blind, sipping hot cocoa laced with vanilla schnapps, and wait for birds on the wing. It would only be a few hours. That doesn't sound so bad, does it? Sure, but here's how it plays out in real time.

Beeeeep! Beeeeeep! The alarm clock goes off like a bomb promptly at 4 a.m. on Saturday morning. What? My brain assumes this is a nightmare and I'm not really awake. But a cheerful, masculine voice keeps insisting that it's time to get up. My rational brain does the sensible thing and buries itself under the pillow. Everywhere else in this time zone, sane people are getting their full quota of REM sleep. But not me. An invisible hand whisks the pillow away, so I go along with the nightmare. No, there's no time to brush your teeth or brew coffee, barely enough time to get dressed and hop into the stink wagon. Off we go.

We do, thankfully, stop and fill up our travel mugs with gas station coffee, which at 4:15 a.m. tastes like the elixir of life. Sort of. Okay, not so much. Then off to the fields to set up. Set up? Oh yes, my camo guy explains, I get to drag a 200-pound bag of decoys through the snow and knee-deep slush to the blind and then scatter the decoys to entice the poor little real ducks to come check out the hot babes. Apparently ducks are a lot like men—easily seduced by plastic enhancements.

At least I'm moving, generating some body heat. In the dark, I can't be sure how the decoys look, but I don't have a clue what I'm doing anyway. What exactly is a duck looking for when it spies an attractive though oddly immobile flock of feathered fellows? Hell if I know. Then I remind myself that when we go shopping, the outdoorsman goes into rapture just walking past the mannequins in the lingerie department.

Now it is time to get into the blinds. Wait, I am lying down…and I am by myself. How am I going to drink my spiked hot chocolate lying down? Who am I going to talk to? Who is going to be keeping me warm in the frickin' blizzard and gusting winds that are about to carry me and this freakish rat-trap blind away? Apparently you're supposed to drink the coffee beforehand, be quiet, and wear a lot more warm clothes.

Oh, and did I mention that once I'm in the blind, the camo guy closes the lid? What?! It's pitch black, cold, and smells like I imagine last year's rotting corpse would smell. There's a tiny peep-hole, and I can just barely make out a patch of sky. This is starting to feel too much like some B-grade horror movie. No one will ever find my frozen, blue body because who in their right mind would ever wander out into a mucky swamp and start pulling up on random mats of grass expecting to find a damsel in distress? Or her bones in a shallow grave. I don't hear any birds, but questions are fluttering around my mind. Namely, do we have a large life insurance policy that I do not know about?

Little do I realize, but this party is just getting started! I am in the blind, wondering what it feels like to freeze to death, and falling into a trance as I lie on the frozen ground looking at the sky through my peephole when a chorus of honking and quacking begins. Quack! Quack! Quack! HONK! HOOOOONKKKKK! At first, I think the birds have arrived. Then I realize that no living bird sounds anything like this—it's just the camo guy pretending to be ducks and

geese. Which is exactly what it sounds like. Then an eerie silence…
we are waiting for the poor little waterfowl to wander by on this
lovely Saturday morning. More artificial quacking. Then, off in the
distance, a reply! I peer through my peephole and, sure enough, the
ducks are coming in! Awww, don't they look so confident in their
vee formation? I can hear them quacking merrily among themselves
as they approach their plastic friends on the ground. My outdoorsman quacks and coos, working hard to earn their trust, persuading
them that the plastic friends scattered over the marsh are indeed
friends. I think that they are buying it. They come closer and closer
until I can see the beautiful markings on their wings, the flash of
yellow feet. I think, this is not so bad. It's peaceful out here in the
fresh air listening to the ducks cooing as they—BAM! BAM! BAM!
BAM! BAM!

Holy crap! My ears are ringing, the outdoorsman is yelling commands at the dog, and the once-peaceful little ducks are raining to
the ground. I watch in silent shock as the dog finishes off any poor
suckers that weren't quite dead from the ass full of lead they just got,
and the outdoorsman hoots and hollers in glee. The outdoorsman
commands the dog back to his crate and looks at me, whispering
excitedly, "Wasn't that awesome?" Well, it turns out he's not whispering, he's shouting, but my ears are still echoing with the shotgun
blasts so it's like the whole world of sounds is smothered in plastic
wrap. I can see the outdoorsman mouthing words, but I hear them
only in my imagination. My lip-reading skills aren't the best, but he's
clearly excited about reducing the local duck population. I'm not
sure I agree, but then, just like that, he slams shut the trapdoor and
I'm in the dark again. Time for more mass murder. I love the smell
of gunpowder in the morning. . . .

After four more rounds of suckering ducks to their demise, I'm
wondering how much more of this I can take. I am blue from head
to toe, my eyelashes have frozen together, and I'm sporting some
lovely snotcicles. More worrisome—I can no longer feel my butt.
How cold do you have to be to lose sensation in your ass? And what
if it's permanently numb? Thankfully, my outdoorsman comes to
tell me that it's time to pack up for the day. Thank you, sweet baby
Jesus! But first I have to round up the decoys and drag the bag back

across the soggy, frozen fields that stink worse than an outhouse after a chili festival.

We get all loaded up and the outdoorsman says, "Wasn't that fun?!"

Well, what can I say when his eyes are lit up with sheer joy and he acts like I handed him the moon just by going on this little trip with him? Frankly, at this point, if my lips weren't frozen I'd gladly give him a hearty "Yeehaw!" if it would help get this show on the road, fire up the stink wagon, and get us the hell out of this swamp. On the bright side, we get back home before any of the neighbors' lights are on, so I feel completely justified crawling back into my luxuriously warm bed, and I'm fast asleep before the outdoorsman thinks to ask for help plucking the ducks. If I were still awake, I would've just laughed and told him to pluck off.

CHATTY OLD "HENS"

Have you ever heard men refer to women as "hens," or gripe that women talk too much? And on the flip side, how many times have you heard one of your gal friends complain that "my man just doesn't communicate!" or that he never really listens?

I am here to tell you that men are as guilty as women when it comes to talking endlessly. Especially outdoorsmen. They will blab forever. The subject matter is just a little different than ours. Women talk about people, cute hairdos, family issues, what the kids are up to, and the latest hunky movie star. Outdoorsmen talk about the size of the deer they shot last year, the size of elk they saw yesterday morning, the size of their dog, the size of their gun, the size of their knife, and even the length of their…fly rod. Then they talk about the size of the fish they caught or didn't catch—oh my lord do they go on about the size of their fish. It must be some sort of male compensation thing. And they drone on and on about what lures or flies to use, what size of lure or fly to use (they really are hung up on size), the glory holes where the lunkers hide, the time of day when the fish are biting, the newest high-tech coating on fishing line, the amount of drag to set on their reels…it never ends.

These are the same guys who barely speak when you call them on the phone. You know how those conversations go.

"Hi honey, how's work going?"

"Okay."

"Oh that's great! I wanted to remind you that we're going out for dinner tonight with my mom. You did call to make reservations at Pucci's, right?"

"Uh-huh."

"Thanks so much for taking care of that! Are you still planning on hitting the gym after work?"

"Yeah."

"Well, be sure to shower and change into some nice clothes afterward. You always look so good in those Ralph Lauren slacks—you know, the gray ones?"

"Uhnnn."

"And a button-down shirt, maybe the light blue Izod, and those black Stafford shoes, the wing-tip oxfords, you remember? And dress socks, not your white gym socks. Mom's really looking forward to this…it's been so long since we've had a chance to visit, so this will be fun, and I know you'll enjoy the spinach manicotti. . . ."

The same guy will call his hunting buddies and talk a blue streak for hours. One year, my camo guy got his deer about twenty minutes into opening day. He was so revved up! That night, he called his best friend to brag about it. He was on the phone for four hours! I swear, it took twelve times longer to tell the story than it did to find and shoot the damn deer! And the other guy hung on every word!

Ladies, there's a lesson in this. The next time you come home from shopping all excited about finding the perfect little dress at the mall, and you can't wait to tell your man all about it, be creative and frame the story in language he'll understand. Something along the lines of:

"Hi honey! I just made an amazing kill at the mall!"

"Really?"

"Oh, yeah. You know, a couple of days ago I scouted around some of my old secret spots, where the best deals are. I scoped long and hard, looking for just the right dress. But it was like the good ones were hiding, hunkered down, y'know?"

"Yeah, sometimes they blend right in, or they bed down and you can't see 'em."

"Right! Plus the place was crawling with other women hunting for deals."

"Greenhorns, probably. I bet they were making all sorts of noise, bashing around, and shooting at anything that moved."

"Exactly! They were taking the easy dresses, or aiming for the ones way beyond their range. I saw one girl set her sights on a high-priced dress and then freeze. When it came time to pay, she couldn't pull the trigger."

"Ah, buck fever!"

"Well, it was more like a hundred bucks—cute little Liz Claiborne number. . . ."

"So what did you do?"

"I realized I had to go into stealth mode."

"Ooooh. . . ."

"Yeah, I waited a few days, scanned the mall map, got my bearings, and then crept in, real slow and quiet. There were so many prints, it was hard to track just one. So I snuck over to this hidden pocket and scoped for the largest rack. There it was! I stalked in a little closer and sighted in, got the dress right in the crosshairs. I held my breath—I knew my money clip was fully loaded, but I wanted to get it with one clean shot."

"Go on!"

"Well, I gave it a steady squeeze and BANG!—the deal went down on the spot. With the clerk's help, I had the dress tagged and bagged in no time."

"Yeehaw! What a great story!"

A SPECIAL VALENTINE

omance. Chocolates. Sweet-smelling flowers. Forgive me if I dream of such pleasantries on Valentine's Day. Dream on, Camo Queens. When your Romeo is an outdoorsman, romance is the smell of gunpowder and elk estrus. If you're lucky, on the special day he'll bring you breakfast in bed. I hope you like gamey deer sausage and runny eggs. Then comes a lovely serenade of elk bugles and buck snorting. If he leans in for a kiss, brace yourself for the stubble scratch. A gift? You betcha. What's Valentine's Day without yet another pair of pink camouflage panties!

Then he'll whisper in your ear about a special surprise. Be still, my fluttering heart! A romantic massage? A spa date? An evening of dancing? No, it's even better—an entire weekend at an outdoors expo! That's right, honey, we're loading up our two toddlers and driving eight hours to a cavernous warehouse full of the latest hunting and fishing paraphernalia. Guns, ammo, camo, bows, arrows, targets, rods, reels, boats, jerky dryers, knife-sharpening experts, fly-casting clinics, flint-knapping demonstrations…good golly gosh, what could possibly be more romantic than an outdoors expo?

They always hold these things in huge, noisy arenas that are either too hot or too cold and jam-packed full of men overdosing on testosterone. So after being strapped in their car seats for a day, the kids lasted all of ten minutes at the expo. It was too loud and crowded, and there was nothing geared toward little tykes. The outdoorsman was already up to his elbows in the newest coyote urine attractant, hearing all about it from the sales rep, so I carted the kids across the street to the motel and sat in our room. Which wasn't exactly the high-roller Hilton. But it was close to the amazing expo, and that's all that mattered to the outdoorsman. Never mind the bed bugs. And the random stains on both the carpet and ceiling—it was like being folded inside a Rorschach test.

I tried to relax. But then I caught a whiff and realized that one of the kids needed a diaper change. No, everything was clean on that front. Then I wondered if I'd somehow gotten coyote urine on my clothes. I sniffed my sweater—nope. So I flopped down on the motel bed and—whoosh—the odor exploded from the comforter. A potpourri of spilled beer, stale pee, and cigarettes. I got up to open the window, but it wouldn't budge. I thought about cracking the door, but there were too many strange, camo-clad men (stranger, even, than my own camo-clad man) stomping around out there. So I turned on the television and flipped through the channels—all five of them. The sound didn't work, so I left it on the cartoon channel. While the kids stared at the pale characters on the screen, I walked into the bathroom and turned on the light. Then I turned it off again. It was better not to see all the mildew and stray hairs. Welcome to the honeymoon suite.

So the kids and I cuddled and drew in coloring books and I read to them in a singsong voice from the local tourist magazine that described all the wonderful things to do nearby that I wasn't going to get to do. Finally, around seven o'clock in the evening, I called to have a pizza delivered. The kids ate graham crackers and applesauce from little packets while I wolfed down a large veggie pizza. I forgot to order soda, and I'll be damned if I was going to drink tap water from the bathroom sink, so I choked it down dry.

The kids and I were tucked in bed, sleeping, when the outdoorsman finally stumbled into the room, swinging bags of expo stuff. He was so happy, he was humming to himself and dancing around like a drunken leprechaun. Except the only thing he'd been drinking was the Kool-aid from the vendors at the expo.

Lucky for me, I didn't need to actually go to the expo to experience it. Because the outdoorsman told me about it, in riveting detail, on the drive all the way back home the next day. He described every jerky booth, every fly-tying demonstration, every archery tree-stand spiel, every Dutch-oven culinary delight. As we careened down the highway, he bugled, quacked, snorted, and honked the whole eight hours home. The kids joined in with screeching of their own. I have never been so thoroughly romanced in all my living days. Every time I think back on that magical weekend, I get tears in my eyes.

But you know, ladies, we should see it coming. It's not like romance with an outdoorsman doesn't come without warnings and bad omens. The little guy is lacking in the camo department, but with all those arrows, Cupid's got outdoorsman written all over him.

HOT AND HORNY

You know what they say about spring…the season when a man's heart turns to thoughts of…oh boy, nothing but horns! Spring is the season of horn hunting. And we're not talking saxes and trumpets. What the heck is horn hunting? If your guy is an outdoorsman, you know. You'd really rather not know, but you do.

"Horns" in this case actually means antlers, which male deer and elk shed once a year—about as often as my camo man clips his toenails. Come to think of it, his toenails are just as gnarled and pointy as a big bull's rack. Maybe Boone and Crockett should have a trophy ranking for toenails. My camo guy's nails are in a class of their own. My once-beautiful legs look like I sleep next to a mountain lion with a bad cocaine habit. Except these claws aren't retractable. I wonder if he realizes how much I love him.

Thinking of antlers as toenails isn't far off the mark. The horns on a bighorn sheep are made of keratin, same as our fingernails and toenails. Antlers, on the other hand, are bone, but the basic idea is similar. Which makes it that much weirder that so many guys get so hyped up to tromp all over the woods looking for shed toenails—well, antlers. They'll say they're in it for the money—antlers fetch big money in Asian markets, where buyers grind them up into a powder sold as an aphrodisiac. I don't know what effect this antler powder has on Asian men, but if it's anything like how pumped up my camo guy gets, salivating over the chance to find an antler, then it's no wonder China's population is bursting at the seams. The camo guys also say they'll sell them to furniture craftsmen to turn into coat racks and chandeliers. Because, you know, the demand is skyrocketing for dead animal furniture.

Thing is, I've never seen a horn hunter actually sell his antlers. No, the antlers always end up piled up in the garage, where all the neighborhood men gather to ooh and ahh over them like the centerfolds in auto mechanic calendars. Really. I've seen them caress and sniff the antlers, dry humping the horny curves. They even call it horn porn. Ewwww!

I admit, when a horn-deranged weirdo (my man) actually finds a big set of shed antlers, they are pretty impressive. But I still can't imagine dedicating months of my life (and pints of blood to the hordes of ticks that live wherever horns are found) just for the chance to rub up against these bony old things.

Whatever the real reason behind horn hunting, it's enough to get my camo guy out of bed at 5 a.m. on a weekend. In his excitement, he always wakes me up too, then acts disappointed when I pull the covers over my head instead of bounding out the door with him. A flight to Cancun? Yes, I would get up early for that. Twenty miles uphill through tick-infested grass and crawling around downed trees and brambles? No thank you. Of course, he's not truly disappointed—without me to slow him down, my camo guy can run up and down the hills like a psychopathic black Lab who's lost his favorite tennis ball. Yes, I've seen it, and it really is that frantic and slobbery.

See, each guy thinks he knows the best, most secret spot where all the deer and elk go to shed their horns. And he's desperate to get there first, to find all the horns before anyone else does. So the night before, he borrows a neighbor's truck and drives it out to some fenceline at the bottom of a mountain, and he leaves the truck parked there—get this—as a decoy to make all the other horn hunters think, "This is the spot!" Then he hitchhikes back home, spends a night unable to sleep, and then sneaks out before dawn, rolling down the street a block or two before turning the engine on, stealthy as can be.

My camo man stays out all day and into the night, running like a fugitive all over the countryside, not coming home till after dark. He's covered in scratches and ticks, with burrs in his hair and a mad gleam in his eyes. That gleam means that he found antlers! Or he didn't find any! And he's itching to get back out there the next morning, like a big bull guarding his harem! Because...horns!

Yes, it's bizarre. Creepy even. And don't think for a minute that those horns are coming anywhere near my silk satin bedsheets.

PRIMAL HOME DÉCOR

hy do guys love horn hunting so much, you ask? Sure, it stokes their competitive fires—gotta find that big antler before the next guy stumbles across it. And the average camo guy will jump at any excuse to bomb around aimlessly in the woods—that's way better than being stuck at home cleaning hair out of the plugged-up sink in the bathroom, or mucking out the garage.

I'm here to tell you that there's more to it than that, and—this might shock you just a little—the real reason your guy loves to hunt horns has to do with getting in touch with his feminine side. That's right. Did you know that he even has a feminine side? Yep, even if it's nearly invisible under all that chin stubble and back hair (doesn't he know there's a wax for that?), your man prides himself on his flair for interior design.

Okay, okay, get up off the floor, untangle your knickers, and quit laughing for a second. I know I just said "your man" and "interior design" in the same breath, and yes, I am still talking about your camo man. Let me explain.

A man's home, as the saying goes, is his castle, and the walls of that castle are perfect—so runs male reasoning—for showing off the spoils of victory. What better use of that blank canvas over the dining room table, that expanse of semi-gloss sea foam above the sofa? Why, any kitchen would be incomplete without the forked tines of a mule deer's bony protuberances. The bathroom? Perfect for an elkhorn toilet paper holder. And what bed needs a headboard when you can have an actual head, antlers and all, looming over the pillows?

Ladies, I'll warn you, stock up now on art print posters and dig your grandma's watercolors out of the attic. If you leave any empty space on your walls or shelves, your camo guy will fill it with horns, antlers, teeth, even whole skulls, until home sweet home looks like a scene out of *Texas Chainsaw Massacre*. And once that horn is nestled in its prominent home on your walls, there is no going back. You may think you can sneak the bony thing out to the garbage under cover of night, but he will notice if it goes missing. If the dog doesn't drag it back into the house, your man will. And this time, he'll physically bolt the damn thing to the studs behind the drywall.

If you think I'm joking, think again. Have you seen the way men fondle shed horns? They rub them, caress the curves, cradle the beams like a newborn, nothing but pure love radiating in their shining eyes. I'm telling you now, if you're not proactive, you'll end up with antler cabinet knobs, bone door handles, and skull wall sconces. Your formal dining room will never make it into *Better Homes and Gardens* with that moose-antler chandelier dangling from the ceiling.

There's a deeper, even more disturbing side to this. It's bad enough having a room full of dead stuff—the equivalent of toenail clippings—but then the guys start to play with it. That's right, your guy will grab an antler from its place of honor and start rubbing it, smelling it, maybe even licking it. Yes, you read that right—he'll slobber all over that dirty, old antler like a cow on a salt block. Then he'll hold the antler on his head and run around, grunting and squealing like a wild boar. I honestly believe the guys think this turns us women on. Oh yeah baby! You are dead sexy! Chase me with that dried-up old bony thing! Pretend to be the bull guarding his harem. That's so masculine, so hot, so…so insanely frickin' bizarre! Are you kidding me? You and your horns can sleep in the backyard!

YOU'RE LEAVING AGAIN?

This is what it feels like just before you die. I am so sick that I just want to pass out for a week and not wake up until I'm healthy again. I can't stop sneezing and coughing, snot is bubbling out of my nose, my vision is blurry, and this headache feels like someone is pounding a splitting maul between the two halves of my brain. The kids are sick, too. Our two-year-old has the same crud I have, and our six-month-old is colicky. They are both whining and crying in agony. The dogs are jumpy, running up and down the hall and barking, which is going to make my head explode. Because all this mess isn't enough, the toddler just threw up, and the baby has a poopy diaper. Sigh.... Whoever said, "God created time so everything wouldn't happen all at once" obviously was never a parent.

Enter my camo guy. It's a Friday evening, he's just coming home from work, and he informs me that he absolutely has to go on a hunting trip for the weekend and that his buddies are already on their way. He cannot let them down.

Oh really? Are these buddies such incompetent outdoorsmen that they'll perish if the camo guy doesn't babysit them? Is he the only one who can spot deer or start a campfire? Will their hunting trip be ruined if the camo guy is a no-show?

Between coughing fits, I'm thinking what'll be ruined—permanently—are the camo guy's future reproductive opportunities if he ducks out for the weekend.

He begs, he pleads, he whines so obnoxiously that the dogs whimper and howl along with him, which jumpstarts the kids crying again. I give him the evil eye—a withering look of scorn so severe that his hands move instinctively to cover his groin. Then he comes up with a "compromise" that he promises will make us both happy. Unless he's discovered a miracle cure for the flu, "happy" is not in my vocabulary. He'll get the kids settled into bed tonight and then head out, roll into camp and catch a quick nap in the back of the truck before the guys roll out of their sleeping bags. With any luck, he'll get his deer and be back before sunset.

I know that once he leaves, he won't return till late Sunday and I'll be stuck taking care of the kids, the dogs, the cats, and the vile snot demons hosting a frat party in my sinuses. But part of me is so relieved to let someone else deal with the kids, even for just a few hours, that I nod my head in agreement. I secretly hope he asks me to make him a meal for the trip. I'm thinking a delicious batch of gooey chocolate chip cookies. Made with love. Laced with a special ingredient that will have the whole crew squatting in the bushes for the entire weekend. Mwuhahahahahaha!

The camo guy leaps into action—he actually changes a diaper! Will wonders never cease! But then his priorities shift toward throwing hunting gear into the truck and filling a cooler with beer (enough for a whole weekend) and turning the house upside down looking for his favorite camo hunting cap. He finally finds it, on the dashboard of his truck (duh!), and then hurries through giving the toddler a bath and warming up a bottle for the baby. They're in bed lickety-split, and I'm guessing the older one has never heard the three little pigs defeat the big bad wolf (camo guy's favorite story) so quickly. Then he gives me a quick peck on the forehead and bam! He's out the door. Unfortunately, I did not have time to bake any cookies.

There are no words for the intense irritation I feel toward him as I hear the truck peel out of the driveway. He's lucky he's out of harm's reach already or he'd be guarding the family jewels again. It's okay honey, go have your fun. Don't worry about little ol' me. I'm on my deathbed, but I'll take care of your offspring, your dogs, your household. And I sincerely hope you catch this snot plague, and when you do, I'll be on the first plane to Hawaii, alone.

PIPE DREAMS

I t's time to have a conversation that might push your buttons a bit. It's a topic that hits close to home for most women, a raw nerve where we've all been poked with a needle one too many times.

Do you live in constant fear that you're going to have to move into a cardboard box and survive on ramen noodles and water because your camo guy is going to quit his day job and chase his miracle dream career? You know, that perfect job that will allow him to (1) wear camo, (2) not shower or shave, (3) get tax write-offs for 4-wheelers, campers, big trucks, guns, camo, more camo, fishing tackle, and hunting supplies, (4) go on dream hunts around the world with tags for only the most exotic critters, (5) hunt or fish daily, or at least talk about hunting or fishing daily, (6) run naked through the forest wearing only a Daniel Boone raccoon-hide hat, and last but not least, (7) (he calls it relaxing, I call it gross) the freedom to fart in the wind, poop in bushes, and do farmer snot blows. In other words, not your typical nine-to-five office job.

I hear about these magical opportunities at least once a month. Yes, it would be amazing if he could fulfill his dreams and still support our young family in a manner befitting twenty-first-century humans. Yes, weekends are too short. No, I do not want to move with the kids into a lean-to made of pine branches and moss. Sorry, honey!

His ideas for this dream job are endless. I wish his to-do list around the house was as creative. Here are his ideas from last week:

Pest and rodent removal

Importing and wholesaling fishing gear

Hosting a hunting show on television

Sasquatch hunting

Writing and selling funny, hunting-oriented bumper stickers

The list goes on and on. What cracks me up is when you listen to a group of camo guys work themselves into an all-out, near-hysterical, delusional frenzy over these kinds of career plans. "These are the best ideas ever! Gen-yoo-wine winners!" And they all want a piece of the pie. "Yeah dude, we're gonna make millions! We'll get paid to hunt and fish, and we'll be rich, and just think of the tax write-offs, just think of the wild hunts! Whoop! We'll need a new truck—just buy it! Whoop! We'll need matching stealth 4-wheelers—pay cash!"

If you think that's funny, try keeping a straight face when they explain how they're going to sell the next great idea to their wives:

All the stuff I spend money on now will be tax write-offs!

I'll be able to be home a lot more!

There will be a lot less laundry (because you can wear the same camo for days)!

I'll be so happy, I won't be grumpy, and I'll give you more back massages!

We'll always have fresh game for the dinner table!

This job will pay so well, I'll buy you a new car! A trip to Hawaii!

A house elf to do all your housework!

Sorry honey, but you're gonna have to sell a buttload of bumper stickers to match your current salary, and hunting Sasquatch doesn't pay at all unless you actually find him (and not just your hunting buddy Russ in a bad Halloween costume).

Man oh man, gotta love the dreamers! I hope one day he is able to fulfill all these weird camo fantasies. But I'm not holding my breath. In the meantime, when too many guys his age are ogling pretty young gals and thinking with the little guy in their pants, I'm glad to know he's daydreaming about a big, hairy Sasquatch in a dollar-sign suit.

A QUICK TRIP TO THE SPORTING GOODS STORE

As a little girl, I was enchanted with stories about Prince Charming. I was sure that someday a dashing young man would appear and rescue me from a dreary life of housework, menial jobs, and frozen dinners. He would scoop me up and we'd dine at the finest restaurants, enjoy the best entertainment, and travel the world. My Prince Charming would dote on me, always punctual and considerate. When I first met my outdoorsman, he was all of that—dashing, doting, considerate. He was even punctual. On our first date, he rang the doorbell five minutes early. He whisked me off in his chariot—okay, it was an older model pickup truck with an "interesting" aroma. But we arrived on the dot for our table-for-two reservation at Chez Francoise. Dinner was amazing, and then we were off to the cinema for a romantic comedy—and we got there early enough to have our choice of seats and watch the trailers for upcoming attractions.

Well, the honeymoon sure didn't last long. On our second date, the outdoorsman arrived on time, and we headed off to dinner. But then he said he wanted to swing by the sporting goods store—just a quick stop to pick up a few things before the weekend. We'd have plenty of time, he assured me, to get to Jim Bob's BBQ Joint for a table. As we hopped in the truck, I glanced at my lily-white silk blouse and wondered if I should've changed into something more stain resistant for barbecue. As it turned out, I needn't have worried.

We parked at the sporting goods store—one of those national chains with bronze wildlife statues at the entrance and a sprawling warehouse-size building that looks even bigger once you're inside it. The outdoorsman grabbed my hand and we disappeared into a jungle of camo jackets, camo pants, camo hats, camo bandannas, and camo-framed sunglasses. We emerged sometime later into a thicket of fishing rods, fishing reels, nets, lures, fish finders, waders, ice augers, and tackle boxes. Then we sat in the shoe section while the outdoorsman tried on several styles of hunting boots. I was thinking, "Wow, a guy who likes to shop! I can't wait to take him to Macy's!"

Then we hopped up and rummaged through the selection of tents—the outdoorsman seemed particularly interested in two-person models. Which then brought us to the vast territory of guns: BB guns, air guns, paintball guns, and real guns. Revolvers, pistols, shotguns, rifles, really big rifles, and really big really expensive rifles. The outdoorsman was having the time of his life. Rifle scopes, cleaning kits, shooting glasses, ear protectors, gun safes, paper targets, duck decoys, ammo. Oh my God, ammo. Shelves full of ammo, more shelves than a big city library.

When we finally came out of that store, it was dark. In fact, the sales manager was closing for the night, locking the door behind us. The barbecue joint was closed, so we hit the drive-thru at Taco Hell. If the outdoorsman was thinking a two-person tent would give him a chance to get frisky, he likely reconsidered after hearing and smelling what that burrito grande did to my delicate, feminine digestive tract.

In the years since then, I've developed a theory about outdoorsmen and sporting goods stores. I've had ample opportunities to test this theory, and the results are conclusive. In fact, I'd say they are damn near irrefutable: a "quick trip" to the sporting goods store has exactly the same chance of happening as getting a kiss from a genuine Prince Charming.

If my friends are anything to judge by, all women long for this fairy tale, but reality always falls short. Rumors of Prince Charming inevitably reveal themselves to be just that—rumors, hearsay, fairy tales of mythological creatures that never quite materialize. In the same way, rumors circulate of a boyfriend or husband who once ran to the sporting goods store for a box of .22 cartridges or a fresh spool of fishing line, and, miracle of miracles, they were back home fifteen minutes after they left! But not one such sighting has ever been confirmed and verified, and there are far more documented stories of men who left home on a "quick" trip to the sporting goods store and were never heard from again. To the best of anyone's knowledge, those lost men are trying on camo underwear still, to this day, living off a steady diet of elk jerky and energy bars purloined from the store shelves. If your man comes back at all, it will be hours, days, later. To put it plainly, there is no such thing as a "quick errand" or a "little pit stop" where men and sporting goods are involved.

What amazes me is how often the guys will try to pull this one over on us poor girls. We'll be heading to a movie, and we're ten minutes ahead of schedule, so he motors along toward the theater, but with an innocent little detour thrown in. "A new shortcut I found," he'll say. Then he'll nonchalantly veer left at the next side street, and then roll right, and before you know it, you're slowing down in the parking lot of the sporting goods megastore. "Huh," he'll say. "Looky there." Then he'll look at you over the top of his sunglasses, trying to gauge your reaction. And then he'll start fast-talking about the new tracer arrows with glow-in-the-dark nocks that just came in and he only wants to check them out for a sec—not going to buy anything, no sirree, just looking—and it won't take more than two minutes, or less if you wait in the truck 'cause he'll just run in and grab a quick look and be back before you know it. And the talk is so fast and so smooth that he's out of the truck and halfway to the entrance before you realize he's gone. So you flip down the visor and check your lipstick in the little mirror, except the mirror is cracked and covered in dried dog saliva.

After several minutes you check the time on your phone. If he comes running out of the store right now, you could still make it to the movie before the lights go down. There might even still be two seats together. But of all the people milling in and out of the sporting goods store, there's no sign of "Prints" Charming. Time passes. By now, the theater is rolling the trailers. You think about calling him to remind him to hurry, but surely he's just about to pop out of that door, happy as a black Lab with a new chew toy, and you'll be on your way. Any second now. Those doors will slide open and Prince Charmless will sprint right on over. Now. Okay, if not that second, then this one. You count to three and apply all your mental superpowers to will him out the door…now! Nope.

So you slam the visor shut with a bang and are reminded that this is how the mirror cracked in the first place, a year ago, waiting in the truck outside the sporting goods megastore while the outdoorsman ran in for a quick look at the updated camo leaf pattern on the new line of hunting socks.

Why do we fall for it? Even when we know how the game is played, he begs and pleads, crooning that he just needs one little thing and it's right by the checkout lane, it will take no time at all. So of course, we cave and let the poor sap go in, tapping our wrists where a watch would be if anyone wore watches anymore, and re-minding him that the movie starts in ten—no, make that nine—minutes, and he promises to be quick. And we think, "He won't get sidetracked and make us late this time." Right?

Oh, living in a fantasy world can be fun! Just not this fantasy! Because it's his fantasy! The second that man is out of the truck, you have sealed your fate for being late to wherever you were headed. Assuming you ever get there at all. When an outdoorsman walks into one of those stores he loses all track of time, all sense of reason, and any notion of sticking to a budget. It is catnip for men. They can't possibly limit their stay to ten minutes because it takes at least that long just for the initial wave of ecstasy to subside. Once they regain some measure of consciousness, they then start fondling and rubbing up against all the merchandise. You know how a cat will walk up and rub its head against your leg, then walk away, circle around, and bump your leg with its head again? I've seen men do that to the case that holds all the binoculars and spotting scopes! They pretend that they're bent over, looking at a pair of binos in the case, but watch closely and you'll see them tilt their heads and rub against the glass. If you're quiet, you can hear them purr.

Then they prowl up and down every aisle, handling and smell-ing everything. It doesn't matter if they already have twelve folding knives, they'll stop at the knife display and stare at every blade. Pity the poor clerk who wanders over and offers to help—he'll be stuck there all day handing out every knife in the case, explaining what kind of steel they're made from, how the locking mechanisms work, and what the warranty terms are. Wait—forget what I said. Don't feel sorry for him. He's the happiest guy on Earth! He works in a sporting goods store! He gets to talk about knives all day to guys glazed over with envy. He's the damned knife expert! It doesn't matter that he's only sixteen, a high school sophomore, or that he's never been on a real date yet. He's the God of Knives and All Things Shiny and Sharp! Like King Arthur wielding Excalibur, he alone holds the frickin' key to the knife case!

If you think I'm exaggerating, bear in mind that's just the knives. It gets worse. Don't believe me? Try this experiment. You'll only have to do it once, and when you do, you'll never want to do it again. Go into the store with your camo guy. That's right. Walk right in there with him. Soothe him when he goes catatonic at the entrance from the first whiff of new boot leather. Guide him past the towers of $600 bombproof ice chests, industrial meat grinders, and Paul Bunyan-size camp cookware. Soon he'll pick up the scent of gun oil. Just stay with him as he follows his nose. And then watch as he approaches the Holy Grail of the rifle counter. If you're observant, you'll notice that he levitates about three inches off the carpet as he enters the glowing realm of high-caliber firearms. Some men fall to their knees or start speaking in tongues. Rapture is not unheard-of.

And even that pales in comparison to their reaction to the trophy displays. Honestly, if your guy goes into one of these megastores and you don't see him again for a week, you might have to go on a search and rescue mission to bring him back. He'll be over by the big taxidermied bear, or the cougar forever about to pounce. There's something about looking at dead animals mounted in threatening poses that turns men themselves into statues. It doesn't matter how many times they've seen these same critters, stuck in the same pose they were in last season. The poor guys can't look away, and they're frozen in place, drooling.

Come to think of it, it's the same way they act around breasts. If a man catches a glimpse of a boob, his brain suddenly goes on vacation. Heaven help him if he sees both boobs at once, completely bare. That can stun him for a full forty minutes. Even if they're the same old boobs, day in, day out, they still hold some mystical power over men. Which is really some kinky stuff when you realize that dead animals and boobs have the same effect on these guys.

After staring at the stuffed bear or cougar for way too long, some men unwittingly wander into the women's department. Now this is outdoorsmen's nirvana. It's a perfect storm of pink guns, skimpy camo lingerie, and realistic, hot mannequins. Seriously, if they're gonna put camo thongs and pushup bras on those plastic babes, they should hand out bibs to the guys as they walk in the store. I can always tell when my guy's gotten lost in the women's area—he comes out with a bad case of lazy eye, and the front of his T-shirt is soaked with drool. As an afterthought, he'll hand me a bag with a present—another pair of tiny camo panties. That's my reward for waiting in the truck for two hours. He'll even claim that he was gone so long because he was searching for this special gift.

So there I am, sitting in the truck for an eternity, when he finally leaves the store, wheeling out a shopping cart full of—pardon my patois—shit. I can't help it; sometimes you have to call a spade a spade. The cart is piled high with the strangest assortment of outdoor crap you have ever seen. There's a sweatshirt from the clearance rack in a camouflage pattern but in Rastafarian black, red, green, and yellow. A plastic canoe paddle. A skein of climbing rope. (What is it about rope? It doesn't matter that we have enough rope to belay Neil Armstrong off the frickin' moon, the outdoorsman always buys another hundred feet of goddamned rope!) A six-pack of propane fuel bottles. A camo baseball cap (because one closetful of those is never enough). Paper bull's-eye targets. Foam block targets. Paper attack-of-the-zombies targets. Enough camouflage netting to hide our garage from Russian satellites. A five-gallon bucket full of saltwater fishing lures (never mind that the coast is 800 miles away). A pair of sandals. (It's November, but "they were on sale!") And one pair of camo panties.

You're thinking, "What the hell? Nobody is that random!" Oh yeah. Here's the scoop. He walked into the store knowing he had a ten-minute deadline, so he ran up and down the aisles like an

Olympic sprinter on meth, throwing shit in his cart without looking at what he was grabbing. To be fair, there is some method to his madness. He's loose inside his favorite place on Earth, so no matter what he grabs, it's all good. This is impulse buying on steroids. When he gets home, he can slowly go through his piles of loot and savor each treasure.

At any rate, now you know why Snow White is always asleep when Prince Charming finally shows up—she's been passed out in the truck waiting for him to finish his "ten-minute" errand. This also explains the seven dwarves—someone has to work to pay off the never-ending credit card bills. For your patience, you're rewarded with a kiss, and one more pair of camo panties. And we all live frickin' happily ever frickin' after.

RAMBO GOES FISHING

I f you're like me, as a little girl you heard stories about Robin Hood and William Tell, and you thought of archery as a noble, even gallant, art. Then you met an outdoorsman. Oh sure, he may have courted you with his prowess in putting an arrow into a distant target. But his bow didn't look elegant like Sir Robin's. (No, the outdoorsman's bow was a cobweb of strings, pulleys, and bendy arms, more like some as-seen-on-TV exercise gadget for perkier boobs.) And then he went bowhunting one day and came back with a bloody carcass. Suddenly archery had a grisly side.

Fishing, too, has a noble quality—the stately fly-fisherman in a hat and vest with his dainty rod and precision casting across a sparkling clear stream. The delicate dance of playing the trout as you reel him in, scooping him from the water in a polished, wood-handled net. The careful removal of the hook and gentle release of the trout.

Well, forget all that. In fact, if you have a weak stomach, just skip ahead to the next chapter.

Bowfishing is more like combining Rambo's exploding arrowheads with a splash-filled romp through a swamp writhing in monster fish. And the results look like something out of one of those chainsaw massacre movies, but with more blood and gore. Some of it even comes from the fish.

Seriously, my camo guy always comes back from bowfishing covered head to toe in mud, pond scum, fish guts, and some-one's plasma. Somehow he manages to get sunburned, too. You'd think an inch-thick slather of fish slime would have a higher SPF factor.

So the basic idea behind bowfishing is that you pack as many buddies and as much beer as you can into a small, open boat without sinking it. Then you rip across the lake, skimming right by all the best deep-water fishing holes, and pull up in the foulest-smelling, swampiest, muckiest little cove. Next, everyone grabs a bow, nocks an arrow, and starts shooting at anything that moves. See, this isn't like normal fishing, where you pretend the fish are really smart and can sense you from a mile away so you have to sneak up on them and fake them out with museum-quality reproductions of grass-hoppers and tsetse flies. Nope. Bowfishermen don't mess around. To them, fish are pea-brained, bottom-feeding slime-balloons just waiting to be popped. Knowing they're going to get slimed, they wear cutoff shorts, old running shoes, and nothing else. Some of them go barefoot. They jump right into the murky water and start raining arrows into the muck.

If an arrow accidentally hits a fish, the poor thing thrashes like crazy, sending muck and fish guts flying. A sane person would run the other way, but noooo, our bowfisherman has planned for this moment. See, the arrow has a line tied to it, connected to a reel on the bow, so the guy can crank that reel and bring the slimy, gore-splashing fish right up close. You might as well stand in a wind tun-nel and throw a bucket of shark-bait chum into the fan.

At this point, I know what you're thinking. Disgusting! And it can't possibly get any more disgusting, right?

Well, I'm here to warn you. You see, I went along on one of these bowfishing cruises once—and only once. I thought, "What could be better? A day on the water surrounded by hunky men in skimpy shorts, cold beer, working on my bikini tan." Of course, things went downhill pretty quick when the "fishing" started. I gagged and then ran for the far end of the boat. As bad as it was, I figured each of the guys would get a fish or run out of arrows, and then we'd head back. But I wasn't thinking straight. Remember: the arrow is tethered to the bow with a line. They keep using the same arrow over and over. Which means they can fish…all…day…long.

So there we were, anchored in this stinky, toxic stew, hour after hour. And I realized something. Bowfishing isn't about catch-and-release. Hell no. That fish just had a half-inch hole blasted through his belly from a high-velocity arrow—there's no "gentle release" and quick swim back to the wife and kids. So every fish gets hauled out and thrown into the boat. Where they flop, gasping, in the hot sun. Until they don't flop or gasp anymore. Piles of dead fish. Covered in slime. In the hot sun.

Did I mention that these are carp?

If you're not familiar with this particular species, then you should know that carp are the ugliest, dirtiest, smelliest, grossest fish on the planet. And that's when they're alive. Imagine a full boatload of disgusting, bloody, reeking dead carp. There are no words.

Which is how I found myself out of the boat, waist-deep in the muck, wading away from the boat. Now you would think that a cute girl in a bikini would have no problem catching the eye of a hunky man. That such a man would never mistake such a bathing beauty for something as utterly nauseating as a carp. That there is no possible way her lithesome foot feeling its way through the greasy mud oozing through her toes could be misperceived as an escaping fish. Yes, even the emergency room doctor—who's seen everything—found it hard to believe.

HUNTIN' N' FISHIN' LINGO

It is absolutely hilarious to listen to the outdoorsman on the phone with his hunting buddies. I swear they come up with the most ridiculous stuff to talk about. Of course, it is all about hunting, fishing, 4-wheelers, snow-mobiles, and trucks. One of them could have just heard that he only has a week to live, and that would still come last in the conversation when there is a big buck to be discussed or a new hunting ground to brag up. It is no big deal that the outdoorsman had a heart attack yesterday... no big deal that our house exploded last night...no big deal that we are pregnant with our first child....But a big, big deal that the outdoorsman got permission to hunt on a new private property. Sigh.

When you listen to outdoorsmen's conversations, they say things like, "We're gonna waylay them som' bitches!" Really? What does that even mean? To a non-hunter like myself, it sounds like gibberish. Who knew that the hunting world has its own language and its own rules of enunciation? Perfectly intelligent, well-educated guys suddenly go all redneck when the conversation turns to hunting. It's like their tongues go all lazy. You'll never hear the "g" at the end of present participles, for instance. It's huntin', fishin', trackin', shootin', eatin', and hikin'. They drop other consonants, too. So instead of "let's go," you'll hear "lez go." This peculiar logic also pares many words down to one syllable. Your dog may be a pedigree Labrador retriever, but when he's hunting, he's just a Lab.

To the uninitiated, it is hard to make sense of all this until you decipher the lingo. For example: "I was glassin' a monster som' bitch in the honey hole, gettin' ready to go blast 'em, when a trophy dumbass came stumblin' in, spooked 'em, and then smoked 'em. Man, you shoulda seen the Boone n' Crockett on 'em."

In translation, we learn that this actually means: "I was watching a big animal with my spotting scope and was preparing to shoot when another hunter appeared and shot the animal. The animal had big antlers."

It sounds way more fun in the special huntin' lingo. So it's no surprise that fishing has its own language as well. And fishing lingo—sorry, I mean, fishin' lingo—is just as goofy. Once again, every fish is a "monster." Fat ones are called "footballs." And even though that beautiful fish is a westslope cutthroat trout, we just call it a cutt. Not that the fish cares. No, most of this terminology would be lost on the poor trout. Can fish even hear? I mean, they don't have ears sticking out of the sides of their heads, right? Maybe that's why outdoorsmen talk to fish: they can say all sorts of stupid stuff and the fish never call them on it. The weird thing is, this "fish talkin'" sounds a lot like how construction workers catcall at women walking by. It's genuinely creepy. As soon as my outdoorsman wets his line, he starts saying things like, "I'ma gitcha!" and "Open that purty mouth," or "You know you want my worm." No doubt this explains why fish play so hard to get. What a romantic.

The last time we went fishing, my guy kept up a constant chatter. As I was slathering sunscreen on my legs, he said, "Oooh, look atchyou, aren't you a little cutie!" I laughed and turned to thank him for the compliment, but he was staring down into the water. Then he crooned, "C'mon baby, don't be a tease. Come to daddy!" My smile faded. And I didn't smile at all later that night as I was getting into bed and he tried to snuggle up, saying, "Oooh, look atchyou, aren't you a little cutie!"

The language really takes off when one of them catches a fish. Well, not exactly "catches," because they never actually land a fish, but they do occasionally hook one, temporarily. You'll see the line go tight, the rod tip bends, and then the guy starts hollering, "Wahoo!! I got a monster! She's a frickin' submarine!" And suddenly everyone's on the same side of the boat, which tilts crazily like the *Titanic* but somehow (usually) avoids capsizing.

"Hold 'er tight!" someone yells.

"Let 'er run!" shouts another.

"She's sounding!" roars a third. (How many guys are on this boat?)

"Hard a'lee," bellows the coxswain. "Look alive ye swabs! Ready the harpoons!"

Okay, maybe not that last one. But the way these guys act, you'd think they were wrestling Moby Dick on the storm-tossed sea.

The fish leaps out of the water, trying to shake loose from the hook. Sure enough, it's huge—three, maybe four inches long, way bigger than any of the goldfish down at the pet store.

"Whoa! She's a frickin' hawg all right!"

"Bucket mouth!"

"Goddamned state record, right there!"

I peer over the top of my sunglasses. Are they looking at the same fish? Do those special polarized glasses add twenty pounds? Has the hot sun turned their beers hallucinogenic?

The fish splashes down and dives deep. The line whirs as the fish makes a run, then turns and drives straight at the boat. Zigzagging left, right, left, the line goes across the stern and snaps against the propeller blade. The massive trout is gone.

The sudden silence is broken only by an equally sudden and stunningly loud clap of thunder. I cower, glancing at the sky. Wait... still sunny, clear blue, not a cloud in sight. Then I realize the thunderclap was just the collective explosion of cussing from the guys. They all pat the poor sap on the back and say, "Next time" as they return to their seats.

Not two minutes later, someone else has hooked a "monster," the "granddaddy," the "boss hawg" of this particular stretch of river. And so it goes.

If somebody does happen to hook a big one, bending the rod almost to breaking, then the cussing and insults really fly. Nothing is meaner than an angler with a limp rod when his friend has a big fish on. It's so awful that I can't repeat it here. Seriously. ATF agents would break down your front door and confiscate this book right out of your hands. It's that bad.

But as soon as the fish has been netted (or, more likely, lost), all is forgotten. No one remembers the screaming, the insults, the name-calling, or the cussing. They all smile and snap a photo, release the fish, and go after another fish like none of it ever happened. The exception to this is if you happen to be the poor sucker who can't get a nibble all day, then they'll rag on you to no end. For years.

So be forewarned. If you hang around an outdoorsman long enough, the cussing and lovely vernacular will rub off. You too will lose your "ing" endings. I guarantee this transformation is not something that would make your old English teacher proud. But don't worry if you start to sound a little bit redneck—no one in polite society will know what the hell you're talking about anyway. And if they do understand what you're saying, then you've found a new friend, someone else who can appreciate what life is like when it's full of huntin' and fishin'.

BED, BATH, & BODIES

I am a nature lover. I enjoy seeing wildlife, from the most majestic bull moose to the smallest hummingbird. I appreciate sportsmanlike hunting and value the hunting and fishing lifestyle. But when it comes to decorating our humble love nest, I have to draw the line.

Sure, I can handle a few tasteful mounts. I enjoy seeing photos of the critters that the outdoorsman hunts. And I enjoy seeing photos of him and his buddies having a great time. I'm glad to know that he's a skilled hunter and appreciated among his friends. We share that appreciation with a few nice mounts and framed photos in our home. But I draw the line at skulls—so-called European mounts—and gory photos. I'm happy that my man is happy doing this stuff, and I let him know that. But honestly, if I never saw another dead animal again, that wouldn't bother me.

So when he takes close-up photos of the bullet holes or arrow holes, of elk noses dripping blood, or dismembered body parts…sorry, I don't want to look, let alone hang them on our living room walls. And I don't want to have to explain it to my girlfriends when they visit. "Hey girls, check out my skull collection…." My decorating tastes aren't exactly *Martha Stewart Living*, but they're not Freddy Krueger Gore Fest either.

Don't get me wrong. I can grill up an elk steak quicker than Rachael Ray can strip the stems off one bunch of kale, and yes, I do enjoy the lean, tasty meat. But I don't want to think about that trophy photo with every bite.

I don't want to feel guilt ridden as I cook up the winnings. I'm just saying I would be happy enough to know that the meat gets from point A (the outdoors) to point C (my kitchen) without me ever seeing point B (the merry massacre scene).

I understand that hunters aren't bothered by this stuff. For them, dead critters are cool. They like the feel of the fur in their hands, the heft of carrying out a hindquarter. They like to poke and prod a carcass, even if it's someone else's roadkill. I used to think that this was a gender thing—that if you were born with a twig and berries, you just naturally liked to squash bugs, fry ants with a magnifying glass, and run over snakes with your bike. I'm not squeamish, and was a bit of a tomboy, so I did my share of bug and frog catching, but I never felt the urge to smush what I caught. Boys are weird this way. Men are even weirder. (It turns out that some women get into hunting, too, and some of them are just as fascinated by dead stuff. I suspect these are the ladies who grew up in a family of brothers.)

So leave the blood-and-gore photos for your hunting buddies, and leave the home décor to me, honey.

SKULL SOUP

knew something was wrong the second I pulled into our driveway. Why is the front door wide open? Where is everyone? Did one of the kids break an arm and they're at the ER? Did a crackhead break in and he's holding the family hostage? A mother's mind goes crazy at these times.

I scramble out of my car and jog toward the house. But wait, what's that smell? Sweet Jesus, what is that godawful stench? Has our septic backed up and erupted inside the house?

I swallow hard and stick my head in the door. The fumes are instantly nauseating. I start to call out for the camo guy, but I'm gagging and coughing on the pure stank. My eyes burn and water as I stumble around the corner toward the kitchen. Coils of fetid, yellow fog stream around a tall, dark figure hunched over the stove. It's like a scene from a Hannibal Lecter movie.

Then I see it—my favorite twelve-quart, anodized Calphalon cooking pot on the stove, bubbling furiously. The pot is full to the brim with a brown ooze. An ooze that positively stinks. A stinky brown ooze with... antlers. Wait, what? Holy crap! Are you frickin' kidding me? There's the outdoorsman, stirring the ooze around a deer skull in my favorite pot. I gasp. He turns, sees me, and gets this goofy "oops, I'm busted" grin on his face. I don't know whether I'm going to pass out or explode. Must... stay...calm. Cue deep breathing. No! Horrible mistake!

I run outside and fall to my knees on the front lawn, retching. The outdoorsman follows me.

When my stomach finally quits trying to crawl up my throat and I can almost catch my breath, I look the outdoorsman straight in the eye.

"First—where are the kids?" I demand.

"They're playing at Bonnie's house. Sue's watching them."

"Thank God," I say. Then I fix him in my sights. "What the heck are you doing in there?"

"Well, honey," he stammers. "You know that nice big buck I got last weekend? I'm saving us a whole bunch of money! Instead of paying the taxidermist, I'm doing my own, homemade European skull mount!"

He sounds genuinely pleased with himself. Pardon me while I jump for joy. I think about my favorite, expensive stockpot, still sitting on the burner in the kitchen, that sickly brown ooze seeping into every tiny pore in its nonstick surface. I try to stifle a sob. It's times like these that the outdoorsman is damn lucky I don't have a concealed carry permit. I make a mental note to do something about that, and soon.

They call it a "European mount" to make it sound chic and trendy. What it really means is they want to hang a freaky, bare-bones deer skull on your living room wall. Because, you know, dead critters aren't creepy enough, now we have to use their skulls as home décor. What? Are we the Addams Family now?

If these skulls have a rightful place in the world, it's probably inside the frickin' head of the frickin' deer, with its skin still intact, roaming around the forest, munching on daisies. If some macho hunter absolutely has to hang the skull somewhere, let it be in his man cave, or maybe on a wall in the garage. Not inside the house!

So, anyway. The camo guy scurries back to the kitchen to stir his foul concoction. I run around opening windows, turning on fans, doing anything I can to waft that reek out of the house. But I've underestimated how long it takes to boil the hair off a skull. In fact, he has to keep adding water to the mix because the hide and hair coagulate as the thing cooks down, and the ooze solidifies into a thick, pungent gunk. The steamy aroma permeates the house. It occurs to me that we'll have to replace the carpet, maybe even repaint the walls and ceiling. I wonder if homeowner's insurance covers self-inflicted deer skull soup. But as the stench wriggles its way into the very floorboards and drywall, I realize this is more on the scale of "acts of God." Besides, no claims agent would come near the house now, not even in a hazmat suit.

I can't take it anymore. I grab a change of clothes and lock myself in the bathroom. I shove the throw rug under the door, filling the gap. I turn on the ceiling fan, light the candle on the back of the toilet, spray room freshener. Nothing helps. So I make a run for the back deck and collapse on a lounge chair. A breeze comes in from the backyard, carrying the scent of the big garbage can in the alley— it's sweet by comparison, and I start to relax a little.

Which is when it hits me that the outdoorsman may be on to something. He could invent a whole new line of room fresheners for man caves. You'd have your skull soup and your field dressing aromas for big game hunters. Mud and muck for fishermen and waterfowl hunters. Diesel exhaust and burning tires for car enthusiasts. Skunk surprise and frothy farts would work for just about any guy. I'm sure men would just eat it up. Um, maybe that's not the best way to say it. But they'd love it. We'll be rich! Rich off of selling stinky-stank home sprays. That is something to be proud of. Only a man would deliberately buy a can of "Roadkill Reek."

My reverie is broken by the outdoorsman, wearing oven mitts, carrying the boiled skull and rack. Of course he's using the nice, floral print fabric oven mitts. He sets the skull out to dry in a wheelbarrow in the backyard, then stands there admiring his handiwork. I take a deep breath and duck inside, holding my nose, to survey the damage to my prized stockpot. There are rings of foamy biological crud crusted to the sides, prickly with deer hair and bits of cartilage. More brown slime is scorched to the bottom of the pan. Seriously, it looks like someone used this one pot to turn an entire horse into glue. My stomach lurches. I realize that if I ever cooked in this pot again, I would smell this stench and picture this hairy, brown, gelatinous paste. No doubt I would taste this…. Nope, not going there. Okay, I just urped into my mouth a little.

So the beautiful stockpot is a goner. The outdoorsman comes in carrying the soiled oven mitts. He goes to hang them on the little hook by the stove, but I stop him.

"You can burn those," I say.

"He looks at me and then, puzzled, at the mitts in his hands. "Why?"

"And you can keep the pot. Just not in the house. No doubt you'll find another use for it," I say. "Just don't ever cook me a meal in it."

He nods, puts the lid on the pot, and carries it out to the garage. When he comes back in, I'm wiping splattered deer skull ooze off the countertops.

"So what's for dinner?" he says.

The late autumn months pass by. I shampoo the carpets and wash the walls. I shampoo the carpets again. Snow soon blankets the mountains. I buy vanilla-scented plug-ins for every outlet in the house. For Christmas, I receive a lovely twelve-quart, anodized stockpot. Plus a matching five-quart chili pot. I replace the vanilla plug-ins with heavier-scented cinnamon plug-ins. The last snows melt away and daffodils push through the soil along our front walk. The days warm and I open all the windows. Then summer arrives with a heat wave and I live on the back deck. Soon it is the end of August and something in our garage reeks. Maybe a mouse died in the stack of old newspapers? Or did we leave a full garbage bag somewhere? I poke around, looking for the source of the smell. Nothing. I tell the outdoorsman that we have to figure it out and he agrees. Maybe a squirrel got into the eaves and died there, he suggests. Sure. Whatever. Just find it and remove it before I hurl all over the place. He searches. Nothing. Days go by. It's not getting any better, and now it's like the stink has infiltrated my mind. So when Sunday morning comes around and the outdoorsman is sprawled on the sofa in thrall of some program on the hunting channel, I stroll over and turn the television off.

"Find the stink," I say.

He goes out to the garage and investigates. I hear him out there banging around, moving stuff. It goes on and on. I go stand in the driveway, watching as he sorts through piles of hunting and fishing equipment. Then he moves the lawnmower and stiffens up, like a

94

dog on a pheasant. I peer around. There, in a dark corner by the weed whacker, blending into the shadows, sits a crusty, black anodized, twelve-quart Calphalon stockpot. The skull pot.

The outdoorsman picks it up and brings it to the driveway. He sets it down and then opens the lid. Bingo! It's like the world's biggest, deadliest stink bomb just exploded right under our noses. He slams the lid back on the pot, groans, and turns toward me. But I'm already at the far end of the driveway, deciding which way I want to go for a nice, long walk this morning. I wave at him with a smile and stride off.

Apparently, back in the fall, he was so distracted by his European mount drying in the wheelbarrow, he plumb forgot about the pot full of "broth" sitting in the garage. So there it sat, for ten—count 'em, ten—months. When I get back from my walk, the garage door is open with a big fan running, and the pot is nowhere to be seen—or smelled. I ask the outdoorsman what has become of my favorite cookpot. He sheepishly explains that there was no possible way to clean it. He couldn't even stomach having the lid off long enough to think about scraping out the gunk. For the owner of the stink wagon, that's saying something. It occurred to him to maybe blast it with the hose from a distance, but then there'd be stench splattered all over. And then we'd have every dog in the neighborhood rolling in our yard. Or coyotes. And bears. So he wrapped it in a garbage bag and threw it in the can out in the alley. My favorite, prized, beautiful stockpot.

Funny enough, the cleaned skull and antlers never made it into the house. The outdoorsman never even mentioned the possibility. That European mount sure dresses up the doghouse though.

HUNTING CAMP FASHION: ALL BETS ARE OFF

Outdoorsmen have a unique—some would say perverse—fashion sense. Their choice of what to wear usually hinges on the weather, or whatever they fell asleep in the night before. They bond with their favorite camo patterns, their favorite hunting boots, their prized T-shirt emblazoned with a gore-spattered zombie mule deer buck. I'm not making this up. If you try to put that T-shirt in the wash, the camo guy will rescue it even if he has to knock you senseless to wrestle it out of your hygienic little hands.

I present to you here a list of some of the most beguiling outfits I've seen outdoorsmen wear. If you, yourself, would like to see a grown man in any of the following get-ups, then you probably belong with an outdoorsman. If you sincerely do not want to see a grown man in any of these get-ups, but feel you could love them even if they do dress like this, then you too belong with an outdoorsman.

Whitey-tighties, hiking boots, knee-high socks, and a camo henley shirt. Nothing else.

Camo cargo pants, a teal paisley polo shirt, and day-glo orange trucker hat.

Camo undies that have been worn for seven days straight. Oh wait—that's not camo. Ewwww!

Wraparound, side-blocker sunglasses, a wife-beater, and golf shorts.

Holey Carhart pants with oil stains, a monster truck T-shirt, and ancient work boots with the leather worn off one of the steel toecaps, for that *Texas Chainsaw Massacre* fashion statement.

A checkered hunting jacket with the sleeves cut off, too-short running shorts, and...wait for it...clogs. But the clogs are camo (even if they are blue), so that makes them work with the outfit, right? No?

Cargo pants cut off into shorts, one leg about five inches shorter than the other. In fact, he cut that leg so short he lopped off the bottom of the cargo pocket.

A plaid porkpie hat with bug netting all the way around.

Classy, nicely ironed designer jeans, shiny black leather belt, and dress wingtips topped with his favorite threadbare elk skull T-shirt. "But the shirt is tucked in!"

A week-old beard scruff, long-sleeve red flannel shirt and blue plaid pajama bottoms that reek of campfire, and grungy flip-flops. "Who's gonna see me? We're just going to the coffee shop."

White, tapered-leg, tight sweatpants purchased at a gas station (this was an emergency) and a see-through mesh, lime-green tank-top (that was a fashion emergency).

The same filthy, pitted-out, threadbare, unwashed clothes, day after day, for several weeks.

These are just some of the damn sexy outfits I have seen in my life with the outdoorsman and his hunting buddies. Remember: there are no mirrors in hunting camp, and the only people who might judge your fashion sense will look just as glamorous. Frankly, outdoorsmen do not give a shit. They wipe their boogers in their T-shirts and wear rancid sweat rings in their pits like medals of honor. Even when they break camp and drive back to civilization, they think nothing of walking into a gas station or restaurant looking like they got dressed in a dumpster. I suppose us gals should be grateful. When our men look that sexy and smell that sweet, there's no chance in hell any woman in her right mind would flirt with them. And if one of the guys tried to hit on a cute gal, she'd probably call the cops as soon as she quit laughing.

I'm less optimistic for what this says about anyone already in a relationship with a camo guy.... Oh shit, that's me!

SPLENDOR IN THE GRASS

When I first met the outdoorsman, I thought grass was grass. Yes, it is nice to sit on for a picnic, and it feeds cows and horses, but I had never thought about other uses for grass until my first camping trip with the outdoorsman. It turns out that grass is pretty darn handy. So many unconventional uses!

For instance, who needs wood kindling? When it was time to get our campfire rolling, the outdoorsman grabbed a handful of dried grass and struck a match. Whoosh—instant flames. Of course, we used a nice flat grassy patch to pitch our tent. That grass was so dense and soft, it provided all the cushion and insulation we needed. Who needs a sleeping pad? Then the outdoorsman showed me a cool trick after dinner. Beans scorched to the bottom of the pot? Just toss in some sand with a splash of water and use a wad of grass to scrub that thing clean. Handy, eh? These outdoorsmen sure are resourceful!

Well, necessity is the mother of resourcefulness. Or maybe it's forgetfulness that breeds their MacGyver ideas. Oops, forgot to bring an extra pair of socks? And your only pair is wet from the hike in? Just yank some lush green grass and line your shoes with that—prevents blisters and even provides a little insulation against the morning chill. Left the dental floss at home? No worries, just find a nice, tall stem of grass and slide that between your teeth. See? There's no end to this humble plant's amazing utility.

My outdoorsman proved this in the ultimate test. Guess who forgot to restock on toilet paper for our latest backcountry trip? On the very first night, after a big dinner of hot dogs and baked beans, I felt Mother Nature beckoning. Well, let's be honest—she knocked the door down, grabbed me by my sigmoid colon, and bellowed like a bull elk in full rut. I dug around in our packs and found the toilet paper. A single, slender roll. Okay, calling it a "roll" is being generous. Here we were, two of us on a three-day backpacking adventure— I did mention this was the first night?—and I discover we have four squares of toilet paper to our name. You can imagine how happy I was. Four itty-bitty squares. Single ply.

The outdoorsman must have seen the panic in my eyes. Without missing a beat, he coolly said, "Just take it, all of it. It's yours. I'll get by." I heard his words, but I didn't stop to process their significance—at this point, I was fully dilated and ready to deliver what felt like a bowling ball of beans. I sprinted for the bushes.

The next day, we ate breakfast, broke camp, and hiked to a beautiful lake ringed by rocky cliffs. We dropped our packs and got out the fishing rods. Standing about fifty yards apart, we were both landing nice little brown trout, until I suddenly realized that the morning's oatmeal was working its magic. I hurried to my pack, retrieved my two remaining squares, and ducked into the trees.

As I squatted there, I happened to notice movement in the bushes off to my left. Oh God, I'm sure it's a bear! My first instinct was to run, but my fear-paralyzed legs did not run, they turned to stone. Frozen there in half-squat, my mind raced through the likely outcomes: The bear will come to investigate the noise I just made. The bear will run away from the awful smell. The bear will charge, defending its territory against the foul thing I just did. The search and rescue team, hours from now, will find my mangled corpse, knickers around my ankles, smeared in my own poop. None of these thoughts were helping. Then the bear growled and groaned. It sounded like it was in pain. I stared in the direction of the noise, waiting for the attack, until the jigsaw puzzle of bushes and whatever was behind them slowly gelled into a recognizable form. It wasn't a bear after all, just my camo guy squatted down in the grass doing his business.

It's one thing to share a bathroom with someone—a bathroom

with a door that closes, a noisy fan, and a toilet that magically whisks away the evidence. But him taking a dump in the bushes is not something that I ever wanted to see. Some things are better just left private. But of course, I sat there and continued to look. It was like a train wreck…you don't want to watch, but you can't look away, one car after another coming out of the tunnel and derailing all over the place. He did not notice I was watching, or I'm sure he would've yelled at me to go away. Oh, who am I kidding? Knowing the camo guy, he would've just grinned and waved. Anyway, curiosity got the better of me, and I sat there, letting events unfold, so to speak. When he finally finished (he ate a lot of oatmeal that morning), he grabbed a big clump of grass and wiped his butt. Then another, and another. Sure, I'd heard of people using leaves before, but grass? I glanced down around me. Sure enough, there was a crop of dense clumps of broad-leaved grass all around me. I could see how, in desperation, you could wad enough of it together to take a swipe. It still seemed risky—what keeps the grass from falling apart in mid wipe? Ew-www! Okay, I don't really want to think about it. But apparently it works. I don't know for sure, and I don't care if I ever find out.

But I can assure you that a square of single ply goes further in the woods than it ever could back home.

I learned several good uses for grass on that camping trip, but I am eternally grateful that he gave me the last few squares of toilet paper to hoard for the weekend. Now that is true love. And you know what else love is? It's the fact that I still think he's cute after seeing him pooping in the woods. Some things cannot be unseen!

THE TRUSTY OLD NUT SCRATCH

I often wonder where the strange behavior of the nut scratch originated. And why is it socially acceptable? I know it is not just outdoorsmen who do this, but they seem to play pocket hockey more than most guys. Fleas? Poison ivy? I suppose it's just a guy thing. But why? It can't simply be that things are constantly itchy down there.

Sometimes they just give it a little nudge, other times it's more of a tug and tuck. Maybe they're adjusting their boxers or relieving a potential pinch. But how does that explain the full-on grab and scratch? Or the mindless Michael Jackson hand cup? Have you ever noticed that guys keep their hands lurking at their belts so they can always sneak in a quick give-and-go? It's amazing how quick those hands can move! Why aren't they that fast when there are dishes to wash or laundry to fold?

Of course, sometimes they're not so fast. Sometimes the hand lingers a little too long, and what might have been a brief awkward moment turns into a prolonged grope. I swear they don't even realize they're doing it, like it's a subconscious twitch. I can sort of understand if they're watching television and a hand wanders in for an absent-minded scratch. But when it happens in the middle of a face-to-face conversation? Seriously? How do you not stop yourself from pulling a crotch grab in mid-sentence? Imagine picking your nose right in front of someone else.

Going for a nut nuzzle is just as gross and way more inappropriate.
I mean, what would guys think if a woman nonchalantly handled
herself in public? No, not that way. Okay, that's not a good comparison. You're right—there is no way a woman could touch herself that
a guy wouldn't get a rise (ahem) out of. So why is it so disgusting
when men play pinball in their pants? And how come they can get
away with it? It's not fair. But it is disturbing. Juggling the twig and
berries must be a form of stress release. Or is it mindless play with
their favorite toy?

This must be a carryover from cave-man times. A loincloth certainly would've allowed easier access. And something about a campfire—or hunting camp in general—seems to stimulate this primordial
urge. The outdoorsman and his buddies will be sitting in their camp
chairs around a fire. They're bullshitting about elk and drinking beers.
Every single one of them has one hand wrapped around a cold beer.
And every single one of them has the other hand wrapped around
their acorns. Even with women present. Some of them rest it there
easily, the way you'd fold your hands together pretending to listen
to a lengthy sermon. But a few are hyperactive, like they're trying to
catch a trout in their pants. Slippery little devil.

I used to think that guys simply didn't notice when other guys
did this. But then I had an epiphany. It happened at a sports bar.
Yes, I realize that a sports bar is an unlikely place to have a come-
to-Jesus moment. Even weirder, it happened while I was eating a
salad, trying to ignore the baseball game stagnating on the television.
Some big galoot was at bat, and the camera zoomed in for a close-
up. Just then—in a stadium full of 60,000 cheering fans, in front of
a national TV audience of millions—the batter released one hand
from his quivering bat and grabbed his crotch. I stopped eating,
fork dangling spinach halfway to my mouth. I expected the camera
to quickly zoom back out, or switch to the pitcher, or at least to a
player in the dugout spitting a stream of chew. But no, the camera
was frozen on the batter. He pressed down with his thumb. Then he
tugged up and sideways with his fingers. Then in a blink his hand
went back to the handle of his twitching bat, the camera zoomed
out, the pitch arrived as a white stripe, the batter swung, and the ball
arced foul, into the stands.

I was dumbstruck. Of course other men notice. Everyone no-tices. That's the point. For a guy, groping yourself isn't a social faux pas—it's a flourish, a display, the human equivalent of a peacock brandishing its tail. It's a wonder they don't throw their head back and crow, then strut around, kicking dust on themselves.

It's enough to drive a woman to distraction. But not at all in a good way!

FUN GAME:
"WHAT'S THAT STANK?"

It's just another sunny day in paradise until I hop into the camo guy's truck. Sure enough, the standard wall of stink assaults my nose as I buckle my seatbelt, but there's a new odor as well, an unfamiliar and particularly pungent aroma. I ask the outdoorsman what this strange new horror could be, and he nonchalantly shrugs his camo-clad shoulders and mumbles something about spilling his coffee last week…maybe the milk soaked into the floor mats and soured in the heat. I take another big, long sniff—yeah, that might just be eau de rotten milk.

Okay, I know what you're thinking. "There's an awful smell, and instead of running from the truck, she's sniffing the foulness like a discerning wine connoisseur!" Yeah, yeah, I see the error in my ways: something stinks, so I inhale as deeply as possible to figure out what exactly the stink is. Brilliant. Sometimes I could just slap myself right upside the head.

The mystery stink lingers for days…weeks…on through the sweltering summer. I realize that hunting season is just around the corner, and the damn truck still reeks like a sewage treatment plant. In a fit of kindness, I decide to help the outdoorsman rid his rig of this stench, for his sake. And mine—I don't want to have to breathe this reek while riding shotgun, looking for deer. So I buy some industrial-strength carpet cleaner, pull a bandanna over my nose, and scrub the everliving stinky stank out of the floor mats. I decide to do the seats as well. I scrub and scrub and scrub till my knuckles are raw and the lining of my sinuses has blistered and peeled. I take a whiff—all I can smell is ammonia. My work here is done. I congratulate myself for being such a nice person, tackling this nasty chore, and I leave the windows down for the floor mats to dry. I am feeling quite content with my work.

The next afternoon, we mosey on out to the stink wagon and poke our heads in the windows. Ahhh, the first whiff is nothing but "spring rain" carpet shampoo. Success! But wait…a wisp of something fetid curls toward our nostrils. Then a bouquet of un-known pedigree makes itself known. I stumble back, retching. The outdoorsman swallows hard, struggling to keep his stomach down. The fetor is so rank even the dog starts hacking and urping, all the while wagging his tail in hopes of getting to roll in whatever died inside the truck.

What the hell?! I spent a good two hours detoxing the floor mats, erasing the odor of ripe milk. But now the whole truck smells like sweet shampoo mixed with sour, rancid dumpster. Our eyes water as we open the doors and start probing for the source. We find an old tuna fish sandwich that has greened up nicely, a gelatinous mass that used to be a sprig of grapes, and a half-open jar of last year's coyote urine, none of which smell as bad as whatever's perfuming the truck. We're tossing rotten food into a big garbage can, emptying the truck of everything that could possibly contribute to the aroma. It's amazing what you can find digging through an outdoorsman's truck: a beer bottle packed full of fermenting sunflower seed hulls, a sweat- and blood-stained T-shirt, desiccated dog poop, and half a corn dog from last February that still looks like a corn dog, as fresh as the day it was bought. Yes, these items all reek. Yes, I am still gag-ging from the rotten tuna. But unfortunately none of these things reeks like the unknown reek that still swirls throughout the truck. We keep digging and digging. Finally the outdoorsman reaches un-der the backseat to put some rope away, and then he's backing away, coughing and cussing, waving his hands in front of his face like he's swatting at a swarm of yellowjackets. "Oh my sweet lord," he grunts, "guess what I found?"

I stand back. He makes it sound like a game show. "Contestant number two, can you guess what's behind the green curtain?" My stomach quivers. I don't want to play this game. In fact, I don't want to be anywhere near the truck and whatever's inside. Suddenly, every muscle in my body wants nothing more than to run, fly, teleport far, far away.

"C'mon, guess," says the outdoorsman, grinning like a kid at Christmas.

My mind reels. "An old Happy Meal that's not so happy any more."

"Not even close," he says.

"Fish bait," I mumble.

"Good one, but nope. Try again."

"What is this, twenty questions?" I think to myself. "What do I win if I guess right?"

The outdoorsman laughs, then yanks his arm out of the truck, lifting his prize high. "This!" he cries triumphantly.

A wave of pure nausea swells out of the truck. The dog whimpers in ecstasy, slobber swinging from his jowls. I stagger back, heaving, and fall to my knees. The stench hits like a tsunami, suffocating, overwhelming everything in its path. I hold my breath, hands pressed against my mouth and nose, but it's no use, the odor seeps in, soaks into my skin, sours in my brain. The world spins and goes dark.

I wake up on the lawn next to the house. My face is wet, and the outdoorsman is standing over me with the garden hose.

"C'mon, hon, it wasn't that bad," he says.

"Oh my God, oh my God, oh my God!" Apparently my brain disagrees with him.

"I guess I got busy after last year's hunt," he says. "All the excitement over the big buck I got."

"I don't want to know," I plead.

"I forgot about some of the leftovers," he chuckles.

"Really, I do not want to hear about it," I stammer.

"Awww," he says. "It's just my old game bag."

Game bag. Rotting in the truck since last September. It's now late July. I start to retch again.

He goes on, apologizing. "I suppose I really should sweep out the old rig after a hunt. I figured the rancher wouldn't want coyotes drawn in, prowling around his back forty, but I clean forgot about bringing that gut pile home…."

"Oh my God." My head swims and the world goes dark again.

Be advised: one person's "game" can be another's nightmare.

NOSY OLD LADY SYNDROME

You know how some old women like to know everything about everyone? Yes, they must know every detail about everything their neighbors are up to. Those old blue hairs are master detectives. When they're driving down the road in their vintage Cadillacs, their eyes are scanning the neighborhood for any good gossip—a child out on the sidewalk during school hours, a mom wearing too-short shorts, a lawn a half inch past needing to be mowed, or any other juicy tidbit they can crow about to the other nosy old ladies over coffee.

I'm here to tell you that outdoorsmen are just as bad, if not worse. They pretend that they're the strong, silent types, but really they're just nosy old ladies disguised in manly, hairy bodies and red flannel. They may not gossip over coffee at the local café, but you should listen in when they crack open a few cold beers around a campfire. Truth be told, men are nosier than us women, just about different stuff.

Here's how it plays out. We'll be driving down the road, and, as usual, the outdoorsman's eyes are scoping everything and everyone in his line of vision. He notices if there is a new truck in so-and-so's driveway. He notices if so-and-so's camper has moved a fraction of an inch. He notices if a fishing pole is leaning against the garage at so-and-so's house. I swear they notice every little detail if it pertains to the outdoors. If so-and-so has balloons tied to the mailbox announcing a new baby—irrelevant! But if so-and-so's trashcan lid is propped open by a cardboard box, we have to stop and check it out—did someone get a new compound bow?

My guy thinks I don't notice his constant prying and spying, but it's pretty darn obvious. I keep tabs on him just the same. Last August, he got his spotting scope out and set it up on a tripod in our bedroom. At first I wondered what sort of new kinky idea he had in mind. But then it just sat there, aimed out the window into the neighbor's backyard. Naturally I suspected he was ogling Jennifer, the neighbor's daughter, a cute eighteen-year-old who sunbathes on the deck. So I peeked into the scope. It was aimed not at the deck but at the far end of the yard. An archery target filled the eyepiece. Then I noticed the notepad on the dresser. I stole a glance—"Steve's accuracy up to 90 percent! New drop-away arrow rest?"

This behavior is bad year-round, but it peaks during hunting season. The outdoorsman goes rabid. Driving down the block, his eyes flit back and forth like a fugitive's, stealing a look at everyone's truck beds. Is that a tuft of deer hair caught in Mike's tailgate? What's under the tarp in Joe's truck? God forbid he not see every single dead animal that every single hunter took this season. If he doesn't get a good, long look, he screams in a panic at me—"Look! Look! What is that? Is that a blood smear on the side of Bob's rig?" It's like something out of an Alfred Hitchcock movie. Our quiet, All-American neighborhood takes on sinister possibilities.

All bets are off if we drive by a game check station. He won't stop to check it out. No, we're too cool for that. But by God he's taking a visual census of every critter in every truck we pass. He bounces off his seat trying to get enough height to see into the truck beds, yelling at me to scan the trucks he misses, so I'm twisting my neck like an owl and yelling back at him, "Muley buck, three o'clock, two whitetails at nine-thirty, game warden dead ahead!"

This ritual is important because he knows how the conversation will go when he runs into his friends.

"Hey, did you hear? Larry got his elk," a friend says, establishing first-to-know bragging rights.

"Yep," says the outdoorsman. "Early Sunday. Nice six-pointer." Which translates as "I'll see your first-to-know and raise you an I-saw-it-in-person."

"Heckuva shot," replies the friend. "Four hundred yards, in a snowstorm." This is trouble—details the outdoorsman isn't privy to. It looks like the outdoorsman is on the ropes.

"So I heard," he lies. "Shame about the broken tine." Detail for detail, the wily outdoorsman hangs on for a draw.

This same sense of competition and hypervigilance applies to anyone stopped along the road, especially if they have binoculars out. We pull over and the outdoorsman whips out his binos, too. It doesn't matter that he has no idea what the other person is looking at, the outdoorsman is going to glass the whole mountainside "just in case." For all we know, the other guy is looking for a lost dog or following the UFO that just blasted off from the crop circle out in yonder field. Of course, the outdoorsman would never ask. No, he has to spot the trophy elk or the stealthy bear for himself. "You never know what could be over there!" he says.

More often than not, it's just a birdwatcher enjoying a flock of waxwings or a lone mountain bluebird on a fence post. I secretly enjoy this the most—the outdoorsman's sky-high expectations followed by a crushing letdown. The outdoorsman sees the car pulled over, locks up his brakes, frantically ransacks the jockey box digging for his binos, then flies out of the truck and glasses every needle on every pine tree in this half of the county, spotting not a single deer or elk or bear. At which point the other guy saunters over and says, "Wasn't that spectacular? It's not every day you see a yellow-bellied sapsucker so close to the road." It's hard to say which one of us is working harder to stifle ourselves: the camo guy cursing all birdwatchers under his breath as he climbs back into the truck, or me, trying not to laugh at the camo guy's dashed hopes.

POLITICS, RELIGION, AND THE "W" WORD

If you want a friendly, easygoing conversation, the timeless advice goes, never talk about politics or religion. Clichés become clichés for a reason—they usually hinge on some nugget of wisdom that's universal and simply too true to ignore. That's surely the case here, as any number of ruined family reunions and office-parties-turned-ugly can attest. These two topics are toxic, best avoided even by identical twins raised in the same household, voting the same party line and attending the same church. Best to stick to safer subjects, like Civil War battle strategies, words that should not be acceptable in Scrabble, and how long to cook eggs sunny-side up.

If you hang around outdoorsmen, you should be aware that there is a third topic that must be added to the banned list. It's a topic so dire, so fraught with piss and vinegar, that it shall not be named. We'll just call it "W."

The merest whisper of W in the proximity of my outdoorsman unleashes in him a spasm of adrenaline: his head snaps up, his eyes narrow, his pulse races, he starts breathing rapidly, his teeth clench, and he flushes crimson with rage. Next comes a torrent of cussing, crying, groaning, and bellowing. I've never heard an elephant giving birth, but it can't be any more anguished than this. All of that is just a preamble to a great gnashing of teeth, ripping of shirts, and pounding of fists. If children are present, now's a good time to send them to play at the neighbors'. Maybe for a week.

It doesn't matter how innocently the W is uttered—it could be overheard on a television news program, read aloud in a bedtime story to the kids, or as a warning not to "W down your food." Even simply driving by a Siberian husky or Alaskan malamute can be a trigger. Regardless, the outcome is the same. This should come with a money-back guarantee.

The outdoorsman will immediately launch into an epic lament about declining elk populations. This is followed by a three-hour monologue airing both sides of a debate on W reintroduction in which one side always triumphs. At this point, I usually pull on headphones and play a tragic Italian opera on my mp3 player. The outdoorsman's dramatic performance never fails to match the soundtrack, and I'm spared the details of a harangue I've heard a million times already.

You might think that such ranting and venting would eventually release enough steam for the outdoorsman to collect himself and calm down. In fact, it has the opposite effect. He gets so riled, so revved up, that froth foams in the corners of his mouth, and he's so agitated that the only remedy is to go gun and ammo shopping. Which is why our basement looks like a military arsenal with enough ammo to survive the zombie apocalypse. Sometimes I think he says the W out loud himself to justify another purchase. The last time, he came home with a .50 caliber sniper rifle with a spotting scope so powerful you can see the rings of Saturn. "This gun will shoot the head off a tick at a thousand yards," he swore, "and those friggin' Ws are dead meat! Oh, yeah! Dead, dead, dead! Look out fleabags 'cause daddy is gonna getchya!" Then he pointed his index fingers like pistols and fired off imaginary rounds from both hands while leaping over the sofa, knocking a lamp off the end table, and shouting "Bang! Bang! Bang!" at the top of his lungs. When all the Ws were vanquished from our living room, he holstered his "guns" and beat his chest like King Kong. Charming.

The moral of this story is simple: unless you're in the mood for camo guy opera, or you enjoy being reduced to quivering in the fetal position by a relentless thunderstorm of anti-W rage, it's best to banish W from your vocabulary. Better yet, just to be safe, banish all words that start with the twenty-third letter of the alphabet. Just talk about politics and religion instead.

ROADKILL SURPRISE

When you live in outdoorsman country, there are bound to be times when your vehicle and wildlife collide. Most animals are confused by our seventy-mile-per-hour steel missiles, blinded by the headlights, and startled by the onrushing noise. It's no wonder they don't know which way to run, so it's inevitable that critters sometimes end up sliced and diced on the front grills of our rigs. I'm horrified when this happens, but for the outdoorsman, it's like a super fun episode of *Chopped: Roadkill Surprise*. Just like the regular show, you never know what ingredients you're going to be handed.

A few years ago, the outdoorsman and I were setting up a shuttle for a day on the river. Which means it was early morning—the sun wasn't above the horizon yet—and I was driving our old truck to leave it at the take-out spot, while the outdoorsman was driving a few hundred yards behind me in his new rig. I was merrily zipping along, slugging coffee, when a gargantuan buck mule deer sprinted out of the sagebrush onto the highway, and before I could swerve or brake, he ran straight into my driver's-side door. That's right—the deer hit me, not the other way around. I immediately pulled over to the shoulder, upset and a bit frantic because I was afraid that the poor guy was still alive and suffering. I'll admit that I watched *Bambi* a lot when I was a little girl. I have a soft spot for beautiful deer.

The outdoorsman rolls up behind me, and we both get

out to look for the poor buck in the dark. I'm just praying that he's not suffering. By the light from the outdoorsman's truck, I notice that there is a big, furry ear stuck in my now-dangling side mirror. Just the ear. Wait, there's also a leg tangled in my running board. I feel sick. Gag! Poor, poor little animal. Then the outdoorsman spots the bulk of the buck's body in the ditch, so we run over to ensure that he is not still alive and suffering. He most definitely is not alive. His body is headless, and it's a mess. It looks like what you'd get if you fed a deer into a wood chipper. I feel even more sick than I did at first. And really sad. Poor guy!

Meanwhile, the outdoorsman is twenty yards away, whooping and hyperventilating over the size of the antlers on what remains of the buck's head. He's already planning how to display this massive rack at home. And savoring tonight's venison chili dinner.

I have a cousin who has the worst luck with his truck and wildlife. He runs into the craziest assortment of critters. To date, he has smoked so many skunks that his best hunting dog will no longer go anywhere near the truck because of the stink. You cannot get into that rig without your nose burning and your eyes watering up. But skunks are common. My cousin has also run over a black bear, a mountain lion, and a mountain goat. Think about it—when's the last time you had to swerve to avoid a mountain goat on your morning commute? Of course, he's also hit deer. A lot of deer. So many deer that the local farmers often call to invite him over for pie and coffee, secretly hoping that, on his way over, he'll cull a few of the whitetail that eat all the grain in their fields. Of course, being an outdoorsman himself, my cousin doesn't feel bad for the poor little furballs he's creamed. No, he thinks it's a riot. He and his buddies get together and laugh about all of the unfortunate critters that have crossed his path.

In contrast, when you see a dead animal on the roadside, what do you think? "Awwww, poor little thing?" I strongly suspect that is what crosses most women's minds. Another happy furball reduced to magpie food. So sad.

Well, you know your man is a real outdoorsman when every dead critter is greeted with shouts of glee like wrapped presents on Christmas morning. Seriously, some poor smashed rabbit becomes the best roadside attraction ever, and you have to stop, get out of the truck, and inspect the carcass like it's the Holy Grail.

The first time I experienced this, I thought my camo guy had lost his mind. We were cruising along a gravel backroad through a big valley filled with sagebrush. The camo guy was scouting for deer. I was minding my own business (truth be told, I was focused on keeping breakfast down as we bounced and skidded through potholes and washboards from Hell, and trying not to pee my pants from too much coffee, because, of course, pee breaks are not allowed while scouting), when I happened to spot a wad of gray fur just off the edge of the road. I should've known better, but my mouth was in gear before my brain engaged. "Awwww, poor little guy," I said.

The truck stopped so quickly that my forehead nearly bounced off the dashboard, and the only thing that saved me from severe whiplash was the camo guy's fly-fishing float tube sailing from the backseat and hitting me in the back of the head, cushioning the rebound. "What is it? Where?" shouted the camo guy. I started to reply, but he was already out the door and running around the front of the truck, scanning for the dead animal he knows must be near.

Have you ever had a moment when time slows and your vision clears, allowing you to see your man as he really and truly is? A moment so calm, so distilled, that it seems you're floating above him and his very soul is revealed? And did you like what you saw, or—be honest now—did it make you squirm, even just a little?

I rolled my window down and said, "It looks like a badger," but the camo guy didn't hear me. He was alternately crouching down over the carcass, then jumping three feet in the air, arms flapping, knees pumping, his baseball cap flying off, and chattering and whooping all the while. He bent over the carcass, scratching his head, lifted one of the badger's paws, then dropped it and jumped around some more, talking to himself in excited squeaks. Ladies, I have to tell you, it reminded me of being at the zoo, watching feeding time at the monkey house.

I climbed out of the truck and stood on the edge of the road, looking down at the badger. I admit, the thick fur with bands of silver, black, and a rusty tan was beautiful. But he'd clearly been there a while, and I could just imagine what was crawling around on—and under—his skin. Plus, badgers have musk glands. The smell is potent, not as bad as a skunk, but not something you want tickling your nostrils. Unless you're a camo guy. If my guy's reaction is anything to go by, dead badger musk ought to be bottled as a perfume, an aphrodisiac, the aroma of love. But I'm not going anywhere near anything that smells like a bloated badger with ruptured musk glands. So I stayed up on the road while my camo guy all but rolled in that carcass. We were there for another half hour. Camo guy and badger were on a first-name basis by the time we finally drove away. I had to threaten no nookie for a month, or he would've had that badger hitchhiking in the backseat.

If that's standard practice for a dead badger, you can imagine what happens when the roadkill is any sort of deer or elk, or anything with antlers. Oh my God. You might as well set out the lounge chair and pour yourself a nice, tall iced tea. The camo guy will measure the antlers six ways from Sunday, inspect the critter's teeth, and then plot and scheme how to come back after dark to saw off the "horns" before someone else takes them. It's like a scene from *Invasion of the Body Snatchers*, only creepier.

Look, I understand that camo guys love their wild animals, and that they're accustomed to hanging around dead critters—having their pictures taken with the big bull elk they just bagged, holding up a string of lunker trout, or posing their latest prize from the taxidermist. But I still say there's something strongly weird about such a fascination with roadkill. Sure, my gal friends notice it when they pass a big red stain on the highway and a deer carcass off in the ditch. They might even comment—"Awwww, poor little guy"—or think a little prayer for poor Bambi. That seems normal to me. But I don't know what to call it when the truck screeches to a stop and the camo guy is out fondling a dead porcupine before you can even snap your neck back into place. And then you see him in the rearview mirror, holding a hunk of fur, frantically waving at you and hollering, "Honey! Come here! You gotta see this!"

You may as well take your snapped neck right on out there because the camo guy cannot contain his excitement—the sooner you go view the carcass and praise your man's exquisite taste in corpses, the sooner you can get back in the truck and move on down the road. Not that it will happen as quickly as you might hope. The camo guy has to play with the dead thing until he's covered in fur and the dead thing's odor. Be warned: he may try to model the carcass as a hat or earmuffs. Let's hope it doesn't go further than that.

Does all this behavior strike you as bizarre? I mean, off-the-charts weird? I tell you, it makes me wonder, and frankly, I'm a little worried. If this is how my camo guy behaves around dead bodies, I hope to God that I outlive him. Dying first is not an option. I can just picture it: a bad accident, my mangled corpse lying there on the ground, and the camo guy jumping around, playing with my hair, and saying things like, "Rest in peace, good ol' Kristen, Queen of the Camo. Hey boys, look at that rack! It's a beauty!"

Really, I'd rather not think about that. Besides, there are more pressing concerns here among the living. As you may have heard, my home state, Montana, has a lot of deer, elk, and other critters. I'm talking millions of the damn things, breeding like rabbits, and they're everywhere. The tourism folks know that people come from all over to see our wildlife, so they pay these animals to stand along the roads and pose for photographs. That's all fine and dandy until one of the critters decides to cross the road to sample the salad in the meadow on the other side. Well, as soon as one crosses over, the rest all follow. Bam! All it takes is one car to create carnage.

This is a bigger problem than it might seem. According to the state department of transportation, in one year, Montana motorists hit 4,754 whitetail deer, 1,977 mule deer, 220 elk, 72 pronghorn, and 28 moose. We also hit 39 black bears, 5 grizzly bears, 6 mountain lions, 15 bighorn sheep, an "uncertain number" of wolves (huh? are dead wolves averse to addition?), and too many birds of prey and unidentified little furballs to count. And those are just the ones that were reported. This explains why these animals are so hard to find come hunting season.

This also explains why the ravens, magpies, and coyotes in Montana look so well fed. In the old days, roadkill was left in the barrow pit for the scavengers. But that often led to more critters getting hit as they came to feed. So then it was decided that roadkill should be removed: if you hit a deer or elk, say, you were supposed to call the highway patrol, and then they'd call the road maintenance guys to come clean up the mess. These are the same guys who paint the white lines, fix broken guardrails, and patch potholes. Except now they're scooping up 7,116 roadkills a year—that's 27 carcasses every day (not counting weekends…boy howdy, do these guys earn their weekends). Which explains why there are so many potholes.

So now I'm going to let you in on a secret, but you have to promise, under oath, not to tell your man, or any man. Because if this secret gets out, you'll never look at a steak dinner the same way, and you'll never again feel safe biting into that big, juicy cheeseburger. You see, someone grasped the scope of the roadkill problem, considered how much meat was going to waste, and proposed a solution. And so the dutiful lawmakers of this fine state, in their infinite wisdom, recently passed a law allowing citizens to pick up roadkill and take it home.

You read that right. In Montana, if you spot something dead on the side of the road, you can pick it up, put it in the backseat of your car, and take it home.* You can stock your fridge with roadkill. And cook it. And eat it.

But let's not think about that.

I'd rather focus on other worries. Like, what's to stop people who'll weld a big, fat grill guard on their pickup truck and go "hunt" deer? "Yeehaw Delbert, let's go four-wheelin' and thump us a big buck!" It's bad enough that we have to keep our eyes peeled for critters crossing the road, especially at night, but now we have to dodge oncoming heat-seeking Ford and Chevy death-missiles, too. Hell, they'll probably paint their trucks in camo patterns to fool the deer and add side-mounted spar-arms to conk any deer that escape a straight head-on.

Look, I think it is wonderful that these animals can now be used as food in a world where people go to bed hungry. But does it have to land on my table? How about we let Fish & Wildlife pick up the carcass and donate it to a food bank? If the meat's too far gone, maybe sell it to a dog food company?

Remember: you have been warned. Do not tell your man roadkill is fair game. And unless you enjoy arriving late all the time, don't say anything when you pass a tuft of fur off in the weeds or a streak on the asphalt leading to a hoof just over the white line. Especially if you see antlers. Lord knows you don't want to be eating steak that's been "grilled" twice—once on the road and once on the barbecue. And the last thing you need is home décor designed around a wall mount of a buck with only one antler, the jaw hanging sideways, and a look of mortal terror in its eyes. Talk about your deer in the headlights....

*The fine print: as always, some restrictions apply. Under Montana law, only deer, elk, pronghorn, and moose roadkill can be harvested, and you have to get a permit from Montana Fish, Wildlife & Parks. No, it's not a "hunting license." You get the permit after you've hit or found the poor animal. And processing roadkill for human consumption is not without risks. According to the experts, only fresh kills should be taken, and you should remove the guts within half an hour. In warm weather, you have four hours or less to salvage and refrigerate the meat. Also, meat subjected to blunt force trauma is not "nicely tenderized"—it's often inedible. Before even thinking about harvesting roadkill, contact Montana Fish, Wildlife & Parks for the details.

TIME CRAWLS WHEN HE'S HAVING FUN

How many times have you made date plans with your outdoorsman for a specific time and ended up waiting eons past the appointed hour? The outdoorsman's inner clock seizes up when it comes into contact with fresh air. I know you've seen the quip about "time spent fishing is not deducted from a man's allotted lifespan." But they forget to mention that those same hours are stolen from the long-suffering woman back in town. The outdoorsman is out gallivanting around, giddy as a skunk in a dumpster, while you wait at home, pacing, wondering where the heck that yahoo is at. You flip between worried and infuriated. Should I go look for him? Did he get a flat tire? Stink wagon blow up? Sprained ankle? Of course, there is never cell phone service. You swear under your breath that if he's not hurt you are going to kill him. Okay, even if he is hurt, you're going to kill him! I swear, when the outdoorsman's clock freezes, it makes me feel like a high school girl inventing excuses for why the jerk didn't call. Except now I really just want to kick his camouflage-clad ass.

But part of you always worries—the what-ifs are too scary. What if he broke his leg and right now is crawling fourteen miles back to the truck? What if an ornery bear chased him up a tree and then sat down to wait him out?

Most worrisome of all, what if he handed his beer to a friend and said, "Watch this!"?

The sad thing is, after several such episodes, you come to expect him to be a no-show, and you don't worry so much. I know a gal whose boyfriend, Kyle, would go on weeklong hunting trips that sometimes turned into two or three weeks in the backcountry. The first time, she worried herself sick. But right before last year's hunting season she joined a women's dart league at one of the local pubs and really got into it. She found her competitive streak, and realized that her years of tossing popcorn to Pookie, her Yorkshire terrier, prepared her well for hitting the bull's-eye. She was deep into the dart league when Kyle headed out on his annual hunt. It was the following April before she wondered if Kyle had gotten his elk, and she realized she hadn't seen him in months, so she looked him up on Facebook to see if he was still alive.

We all know what would happen if the tables were turned, right? You've gone shopping with a promise to be home in two hours. But the sales are better than you expected, and then you run into friends, and you're all hungry so…four hours later, you're tossing back cosmos at the club with your gals. The outdoorsman? Poor guy, he's home all alone, waiting, worrying, drinking beer, eating take-out, ogling the hunting channel, cleaning his rifles—and happy as a dog in stink.

All of which just goes to prove that time, as Einstein realized, is relative. For every minute a guy spends fishing or hunting, there are hours of worry and frustration added to some woman's life.

So what's the trick to living with an outdoorsman? How do you avoid all the waiting and worrying and still arrive at events on time? Here's the secret—the patented Camo Queen algorithm. Ask him how long he plans to be gone. Multiply that by 2.5. Add that total to the time he actually leaves the house. Then, when the appointed hour arrives, set a timer for forty-five minutes. Don't even think of worrying until that timer buzzes. And certainly don't schedule dinner or anything else for at least another hour after that. In real life, it looks like this:

He plans to leave at 8 a.m. to fish for 4 hours, returning home by noon. So 4 X 2.5 = 10 hours, starting at 8:50 a.m. (he was in such a rush to get out the door early, he had to come back for his fishing vest), which means you start the timer at 6:50 p.m. It rings at 7:35 p.m. Good. He'll be walking in the door around 8:30 p.m. hungry as a bear.

The beauty of the Camo Queen system is self-evident: you have all day for yoga, shopping, getting your nails done…whatever your heart desires.

Some special activities require an additional factor. If you want your outdoorsman home at a certain time from any of the following, adjust your equation accordingly:

Duck hunting: Add another hour and a death threat.

Deer hunting: Add 2 hours and a death threat.

Elk hunting: Add 3 hours and a death threat.

Horn hunting: Add 2 days, a death threat, and no nookie for a month.

Now, if there's a movie you want to go see, or you have dinner reservations at a specific time, or if you want to get to the hospital not too long after your due date, then you should use another patented Camo Queen tactic—lie. If the movie is at 8 p.m., tell him it's a matinee that starts at 3 p.m. Dinner reservations? Tell him it's brunch and your table is set for 11 a.m. And that date for greeting your firstborn? Subtract a month from the real due date and tell him you're a quick incubator. And threaten to donate the outdoorsman's truck to the local PETA chapter if you're not at the hospital three minutes after your water breaks.

LET US BE HONEST

Okay, you've read my rants about the outdoorsman and you're wondering, "Why the heck is she with an outdoorsman if he drives her so crazy?" Am I right? Well, I have to be honest. I am a little bit of an outdoorsy woman myself. I'm a Montana girl, and us female Montuckians are ready for just about anything (you should see the dating pool out here). I can get all fancied up like the Queen of Sheba, or I can look like I just crawled out of a dumpster and all I need is the cardboard sign to finish off my outfit. I can shoot a beer can off the fender of your fancy truck, I can out-fish any city boy, and I can roast up a big, fat mallard before my camo guy's out of the shower. I'm no stranger to hunting camp, and I can fill a Dutch oven with man-food that will have them begging for more. I can change a tire, jump a 4-wheeler over an irrigation ditch, throw a fifty-pound feed sack into the bed of a monster truck, buck hay bales, and shovel snow for hours. I'll beat you at arm wrestling, and give you a run for your money with a compound bow. I can also decorate a cake, run a Cuisinart like nobody's business, and dance jitterbug till the cows come home (which is how we tell time in Montana). I'm a Camo Queen, and damn it, I am good at all of it, and I can turn heads just walking down the road in hip waders.

To be an outdoorsman's girl, a true Camo Queen, you have to be tough and tender. You have to be willing to help him drag his monster bull elk out of the mountains, and then go home and dress up for a five-star dinner with his boss. To be honest with you, I wouldn't have it any other way. I love being outdoors, blasting the shit out of stuff with my shotgun, sweating up a storm climbing some mountain, and hanging out with the guys as we tear down a dirt road with a cooler full of beer and brats. I love seeing all the amazing places and wildlife that the outdoors has to offer. There is nothing better than a hot day on the lake fishing, followed by a campfire, s'mores, and falling asleep under a beautiful star-filled night sky. I love this life.

Just to be clear, I love the outdoorsman. Without him, there's so much I wouldn't have experienced. I guarantee I would not have gone to Alaska and fished on an island with just him, the salmon-crazed bears, and me. I guarantee I would not have flown in an airplane held together by duct tape to go bonefishing in the Bahamas. I would not have gone thirty miles out to sea in a tiny boat to catch a halibut the size of a barn door. There is always some new crazy adventure that the outdoorsman is ready to jump into, and I am thrilled that I get to be by his side for all the crazy, joyful chaos. I would not trade my life as a Camo Queen for anything.

ABOUT THE AUTHOR

When she's not removing taxidermy from her living room, being romantically serenaded by elk bugle practice, or checking herself for ticks, Kristen Berube enjoys a crazy yet laughter-filled life with her avid outdoorsman husband Remi and their three camo-clad children in Missoula, Montana.